Natasha's Sketchbook

A GLOSSARY OF ART TERMS

by Natasha Gray

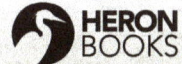

HERON BOOKS

Published by
Heron Books, Inc.
20950 SW Rock Creek Road
Sheridan, OR 97378

heronbooks.com

ISBN: 978-0-89-739236-5

Printed in the USA

18 February 2021

PREFACE

After three decades of study and professional work as a visual artist, Natasha returned to the studio classroom to share her knowledge with teenage art students. What did they know? What didn't they know? What terms would help them better understand styles, forms and techniques? And what terms were instructors using on the assumption that students understood them?

As the glossary evolved, its scope was defined as follows:

- Focus on the core fine arts of painting, drawing, sculpting and printmaking, including key terms within those broad zones.

- Provide definitions for related art forms and media outside the core (for example, *batik, beadwork* or *decoupage*) to encourage further exploration.

- Stay clear of photography, film, music, dance and the performing arts generally, leaving them to other references.

- Give a simple coverage of periods, movements and styles, and within those entries mention some well-known representative artists and where they were from.

- Consider what a student could reasonably expect to run into in a middle or high school art class, or even introductory college or adult art instruction.

- Design it for *studio use,* not a library bookshelf.

- Finally, have it align with and serve as the final complement to the full Natasha's sketchbook series, which includes instruction books on the elements of art: line, shape, value, color, texture and form.

We hope you find *Natasha's Sketchbook, A Glossary of Art Terms* useful in clarifying many common terms and thereby opening doors for developing artists.

Editors

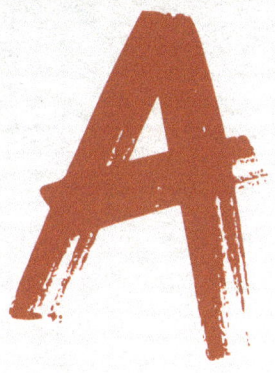

abstract art

art that does not represent objects, people or scenery in a precise and recognizable way, but instead emphasizes color, shapes or marks to produce emotions in the viewer. It became an important and widespread style of art starting in the 1930s and 40s. Some of the most important abstract artists of the time were the Russian painter Wassily Kandinsky, the American painter Mark Rothko and the English sculptor Henry Moore. (Compare *figurative art*.)

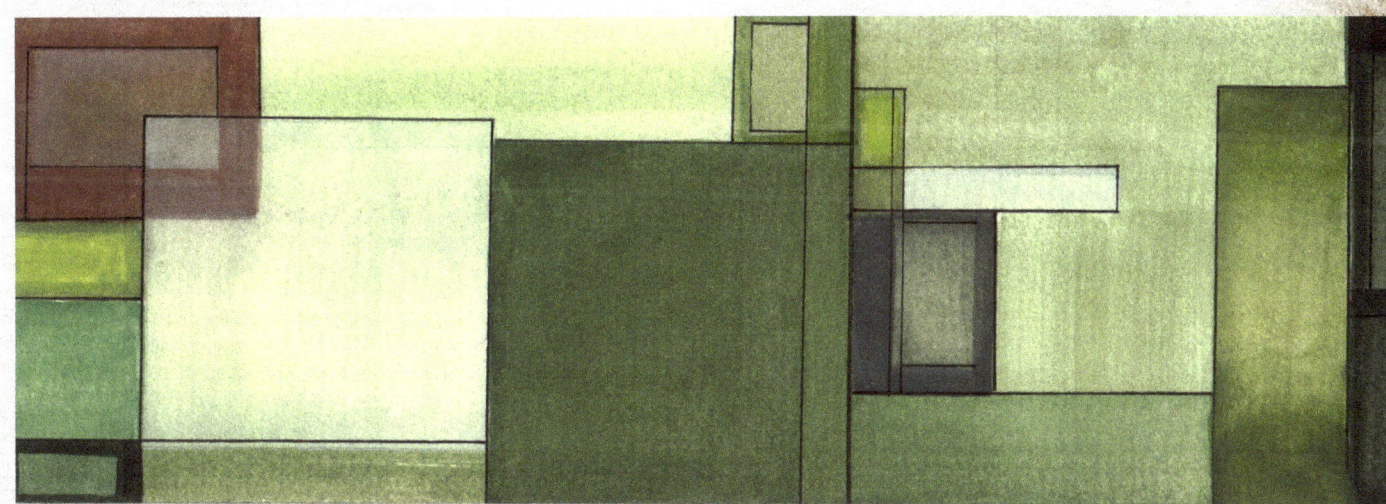

academy

as concerns the visual arts, an academy was originally an artist-run organization formed to teach skills and to help artists achieve high professional standards. The first Academy of Art was established in Florence, Italy in 1562 by the artist and architect Giorgio Vasari. Now an art academy is simply an art school.

acrylic paint

a water-based, plastic-like paint first used in the 1940s. It is made from color pigments mixed with a synthetic substance. Acrylic paints look similar to oil paints, but they are generally less expensive, dry much more quickly, and can be used on a wider variety of surfaces.

action painting

a style of abstract art painting that developed in the 1940s and 50s in which the paint is applied by splashing, smearing or dripping it onto the canvas or other surface. The style puts more emphasis on the spontaneous action of the painter. Well-known painters of this style include the American Jackson Pollock and Dutch-born American Willem de Kooning.

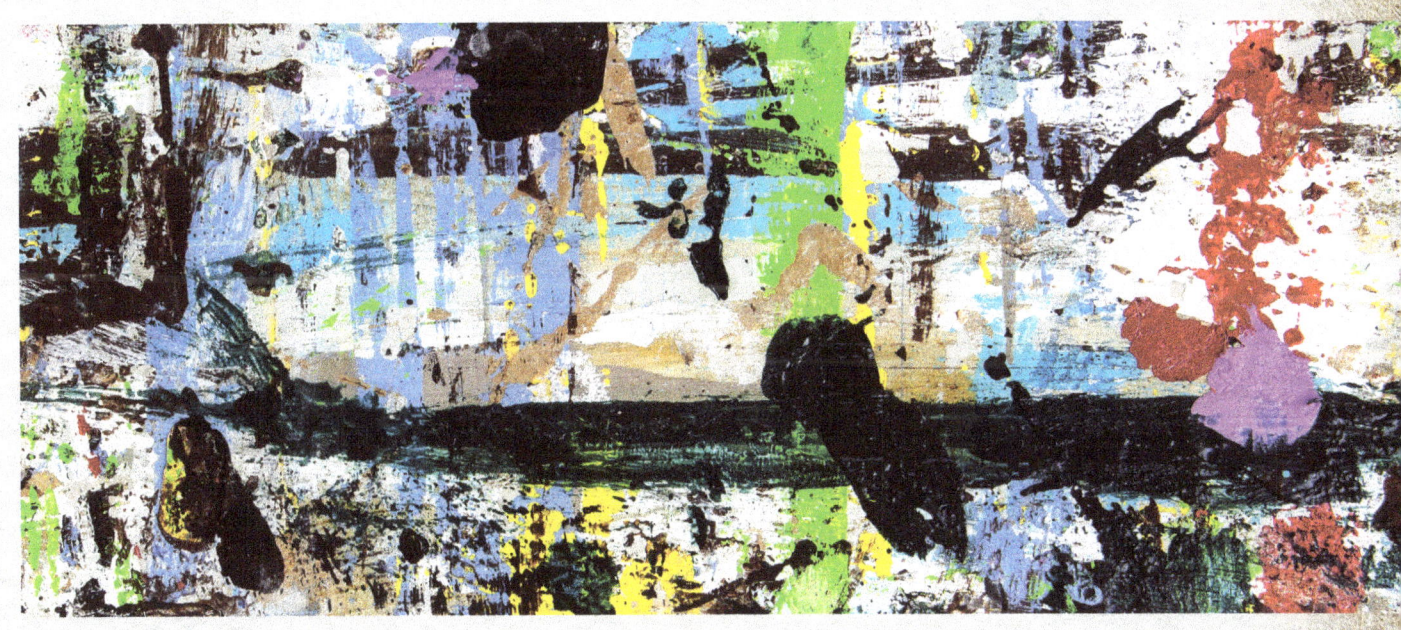

activist art
also *protest art*

art which has a political or social message.

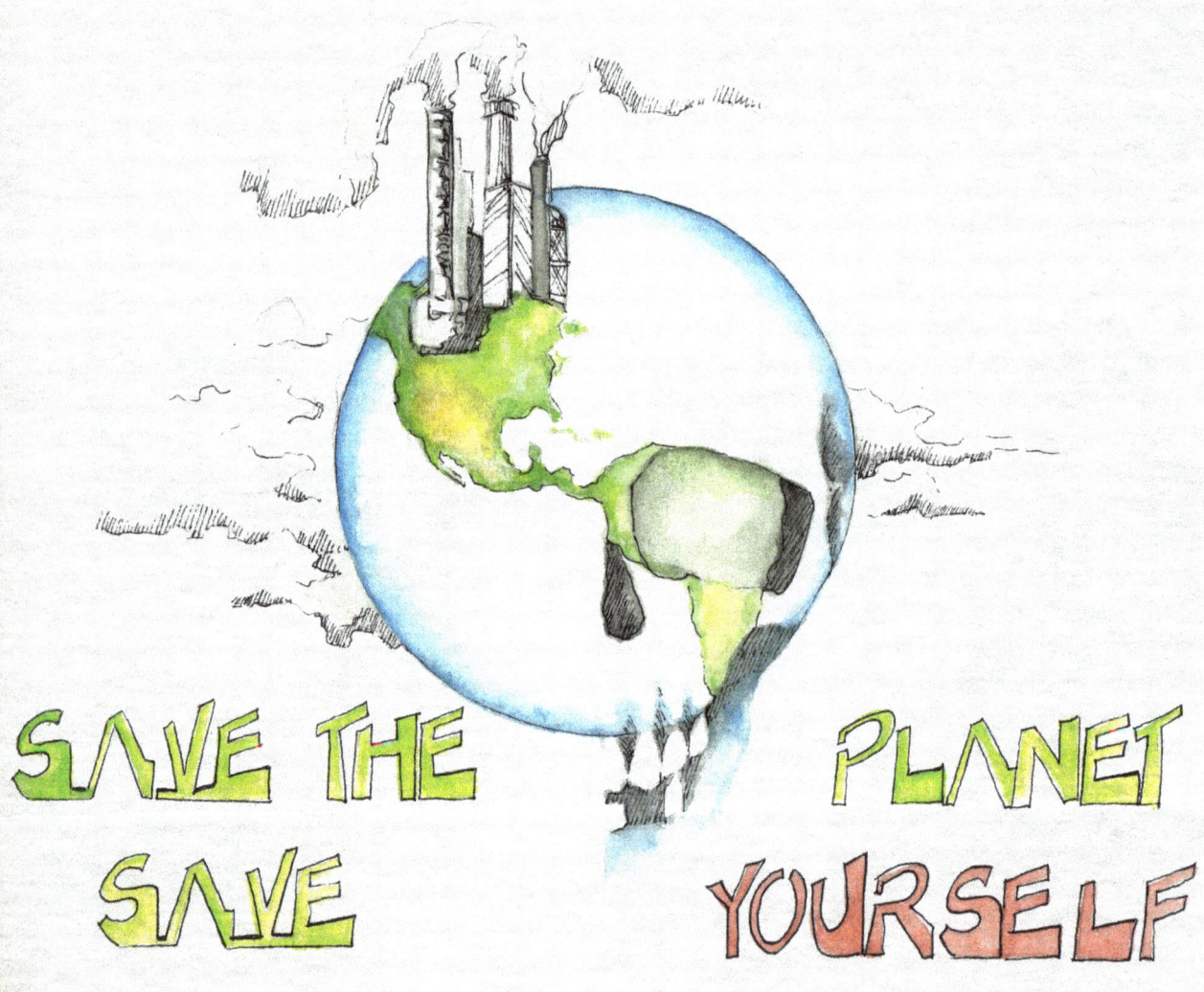

aerial perspective

also *atmospheric perspective*

a method for creating the illusion of distance by the use of lighter colors in the background and stronger, brighter colors in the foreground. Although used well before the Renaissance, it was Leonardo da Vinci who first described it when he said, "Colors become weaker in proportion to their distance from the person who is looking at them." An example of using aerial perspective in a landscape painting would be to paint distant mountains with the weakest colors, nearer hills with somewhat stronger colors, and the nearest plants with the strongest colors.

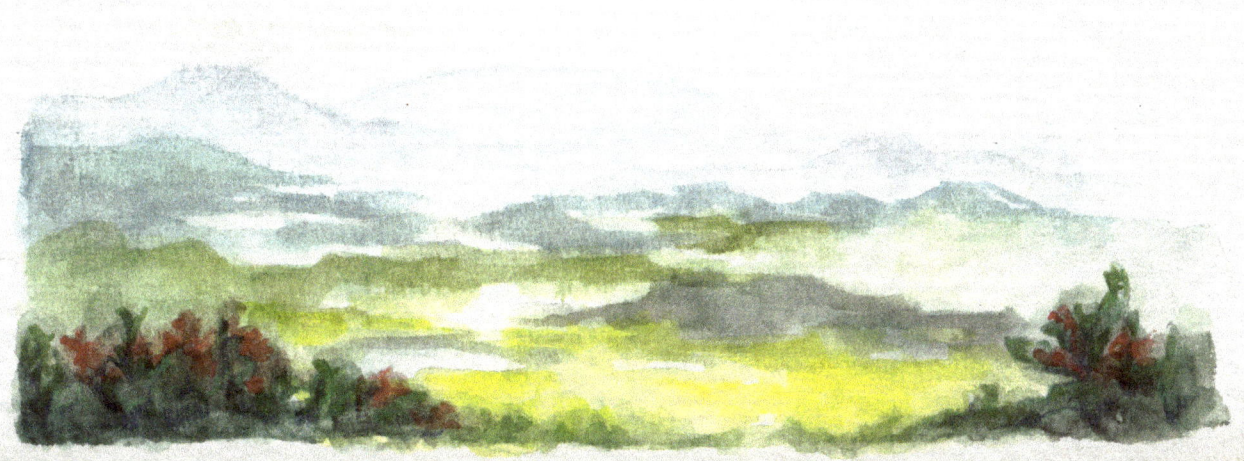

aesthetic

concerned with or possessing beauty or intending to give pleasure through beauty.

aesthetics

the study of beauty and the perception and appreciation of it.

airbrush

a hand-held instrument somewhat like a pen used to spray paint in a mist through the use of compressed air. Interchangeable tips allow the artist to make various thicknesses of lines and closely control the amount of paint being released onto the painted surface. It was most widely used in illustrations and art in the 1980s.

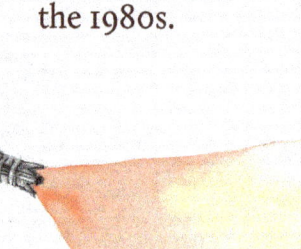

alla prima (ALL uh PREE muh)

a painting technique wherein the artist finishes a painting in one sitting rather than over a period of days or weeks. From Italian *alla prima*, "on the first (attempt)" or "at once."

ambient light

in a drawing or painting, light which is not from a specific source. *Ambient* means "surrounding, or existing throughout." Thus, ambient light is a combination of all the reflections of light in a scene. Shadows from ambient light are minimal, like on an overcast day, whereas shadows from a definite source of bright light like the sun or a nearby lamp are stronger.

analogous colors

colors that are near each other on a color wheel and therefore similar.
Blue, blue-green and green are analogous colors. Red, reddish-orange
and orange are analogous colors. (Compare *complementary colors*.)

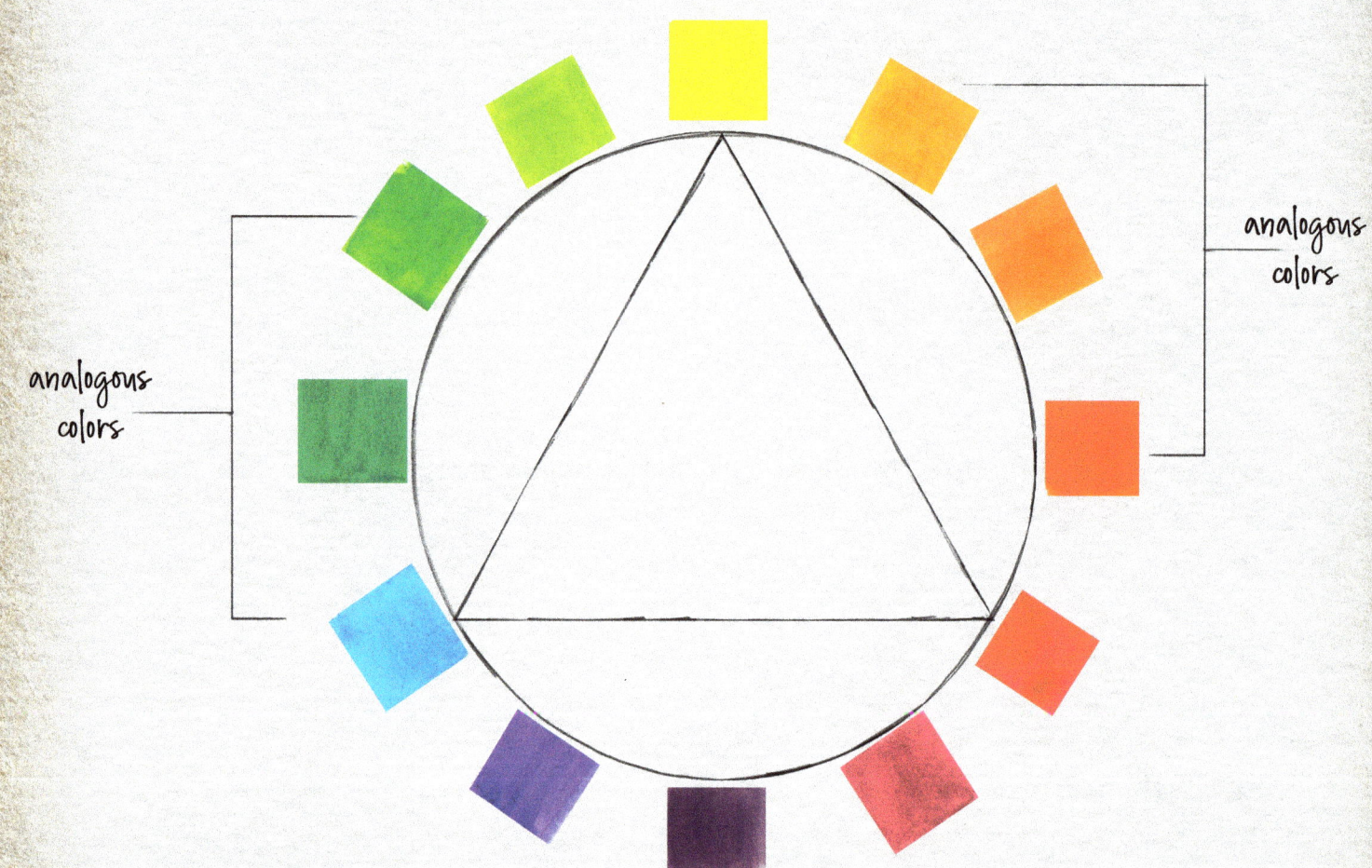

ancient art

from about 5,000 BCE to about 400 CE, there existed many civilizations throughout the world. These included the western civilizations of ancient Egypt, Greece and Rome. Art from this broad period of time is often referred to as ancient art.
(See *classical art*.)

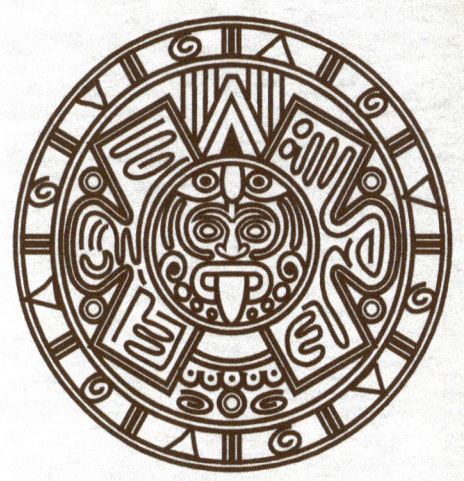

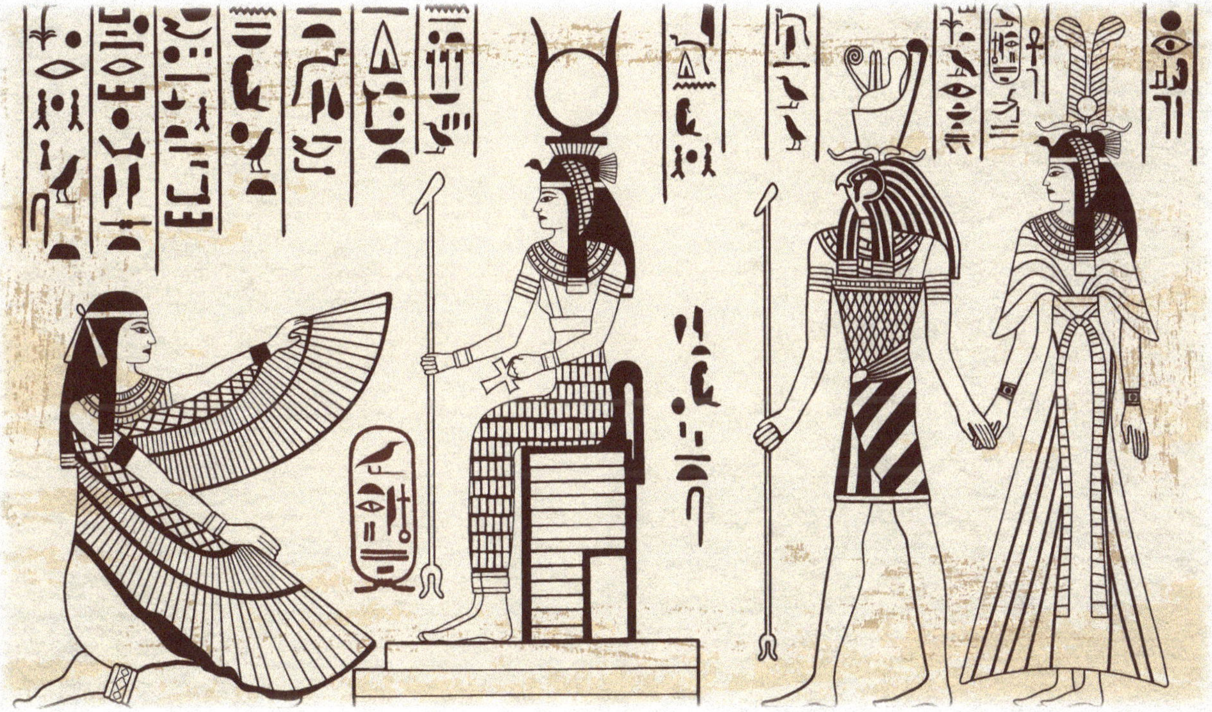

animation

a movie made from a series of "still" drawings, images or photographs strung together to create the illusion of movement.

applied arts

art and design related to everyday objects such as pottery, furniture, lamps, clothing, etc., which are both beautiful and have a practical use.

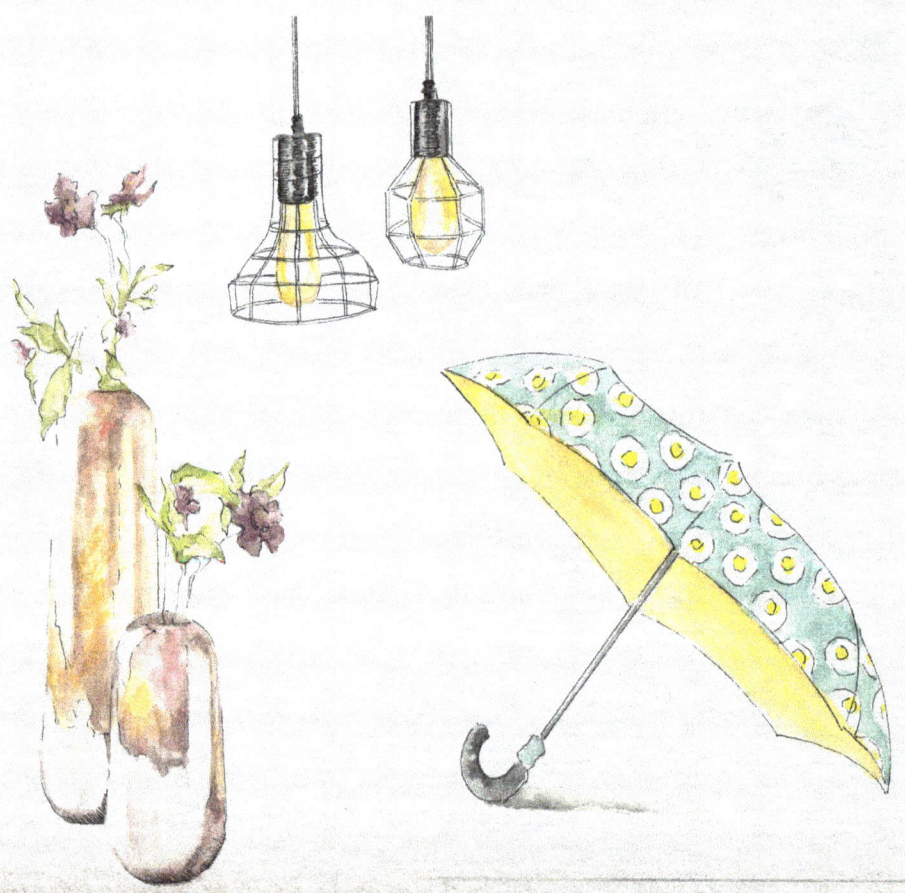

appliqué

art made from stitching or gluing smaller cloth decorations to larger pieces of material, such as on pants, purses or banners, or simply as an art piece.

art

the expression of creativity and imagination through music, color, line, movement, words or other means considered aesthetic or beautiful. Any communication can be thought of as artistic if by its quality alone it stirs the emotions or inspires higher thought.

art deco

a design, art and architectural style developed in the 1920s and 30s in Europe characterized by the use of geometric figures, straight and zigzag lines, symmetry, strong outlines and rich colors. From French, a shortened form of *art décoratif*, "decorative art."

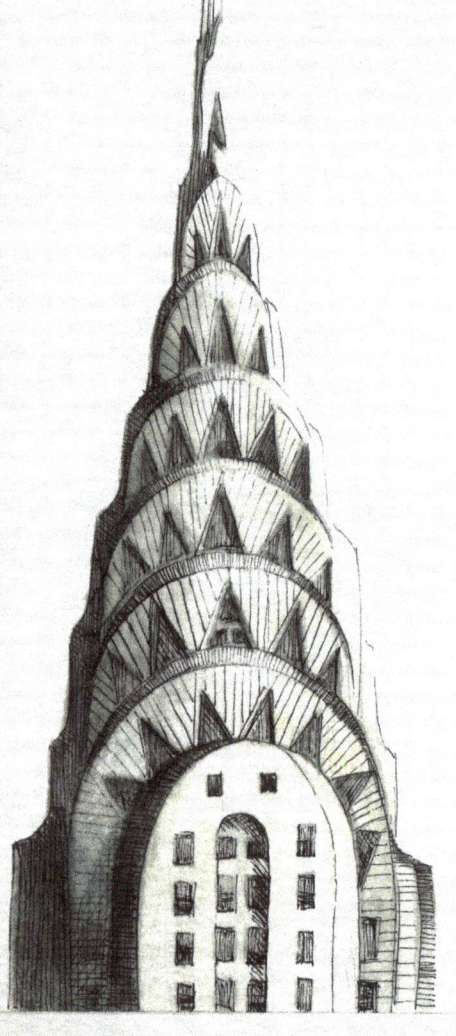

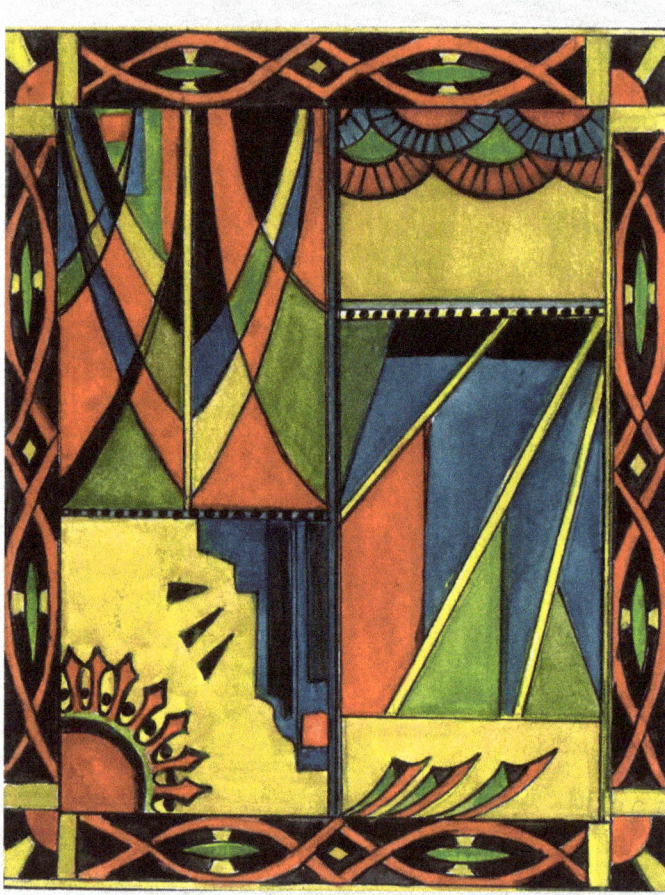

art movement

a philosophy and style of art which is shared by a group of artists during a certain period of time. Some examples of important art movements are impressionism, cubism and surrealism.

art nouveau (new voh)

a design, art and architectural style that started in England in the 1890s inspired by plants, flowers and natural shapes, resulting in art with smooth-flowing, curving, often swirly lines. It was most often employed in jewelry, architecture, furniture and illustration. From French *art nouveau*, "new art."

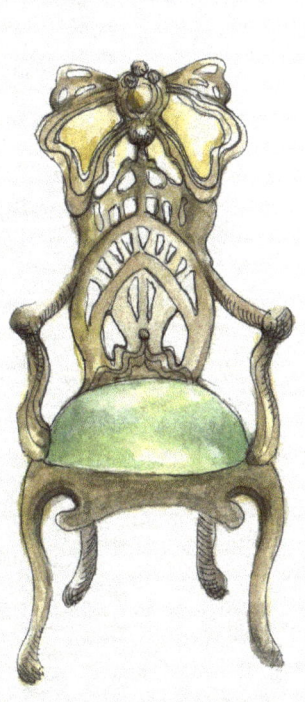
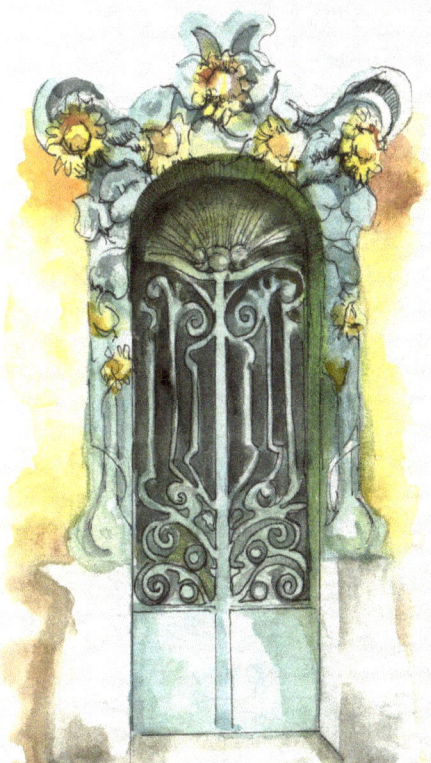

atelier (ah TELL ee ay)

a French word for an art studio or workshop, whether shared by a group of artists or used by only one.

atmospheric perspective

See *aerial perspective.*

avant garde

refers to an artist, work or style that seems to be ahead of its time because of its experimental and innovative nature. A French term meaning "advanced guard"—soldiers going forward ahead of the main group—it was first used to describe art in France in the mid-1800s. Since then, the term has remained in use to describe any artist, work or style that is highly original or experimental.

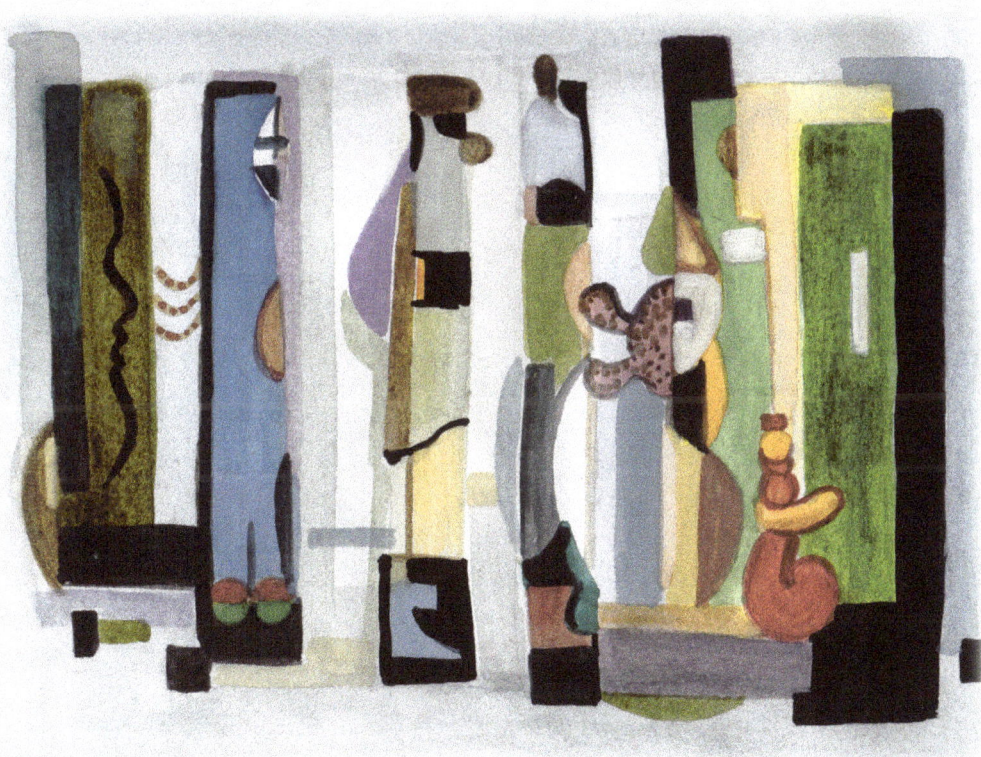

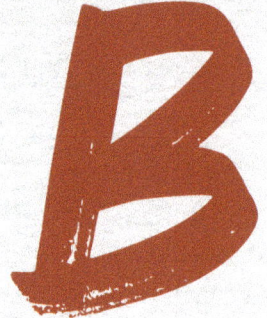

B

a label on a pencil showing that the lead is soft.
(See *drawing pencils.*)

background

the area of a painting that appears to be furthest away and
serves as the scenery or setting for the rest of the painting.
(Compare *foreground.*)

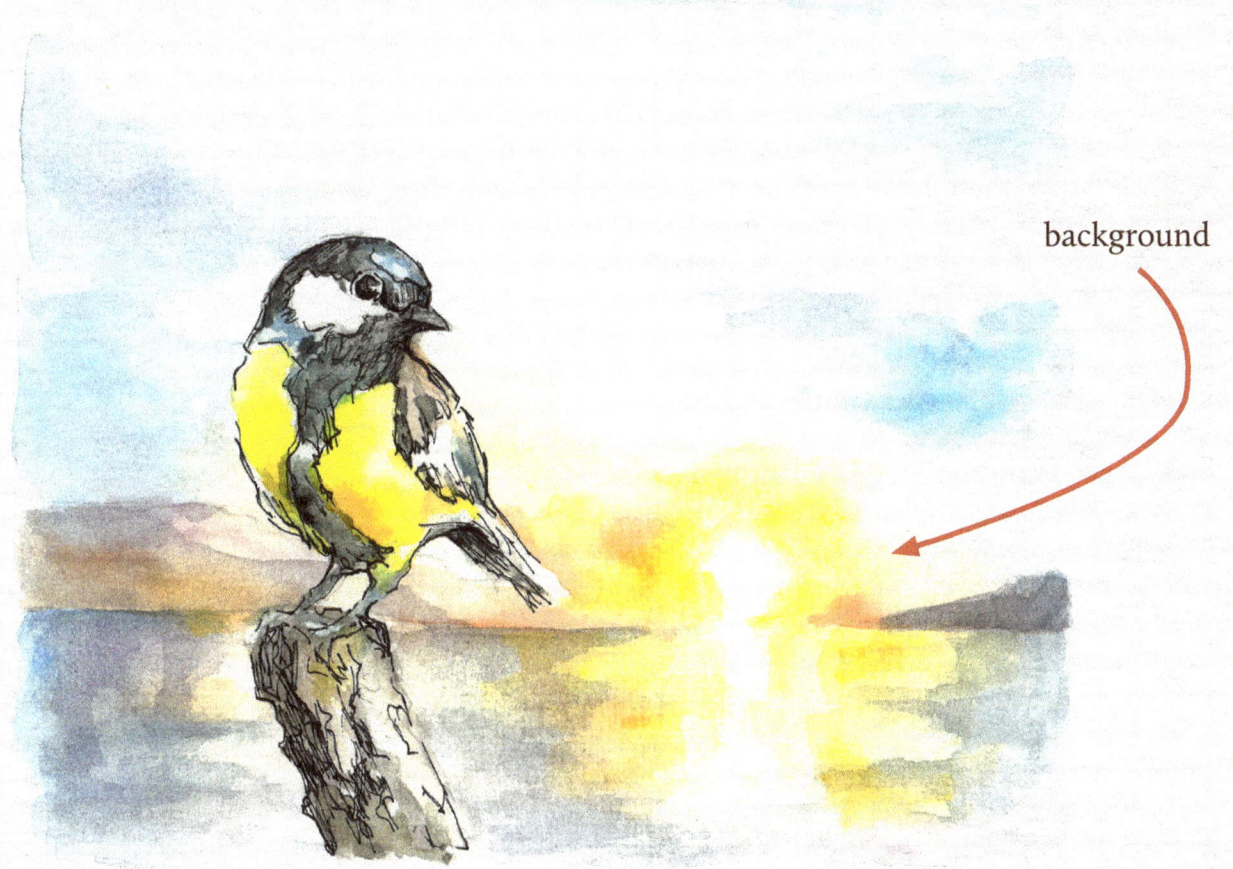

background

backing

a material that protects the back of something. To prepare a painting done on canvas for presentation, transport or sale, it is normal to cover the back with manila paper or a light board-like material. This prevents unwanted debris from entering the back of the framed work, and if a stronger material is used, it can help prevent accidental punctures of the canvas from the back.

balance

refers to the distribution of elements in a piece and the perception of how evenly distributed they are when viewed as a whole. By considering the "weight" of different elements, as affected by their size, color, values, etc., one can get a sense of what effect it will have on the viewer. A pleasing effect is most often created when a piece feels well balanced.

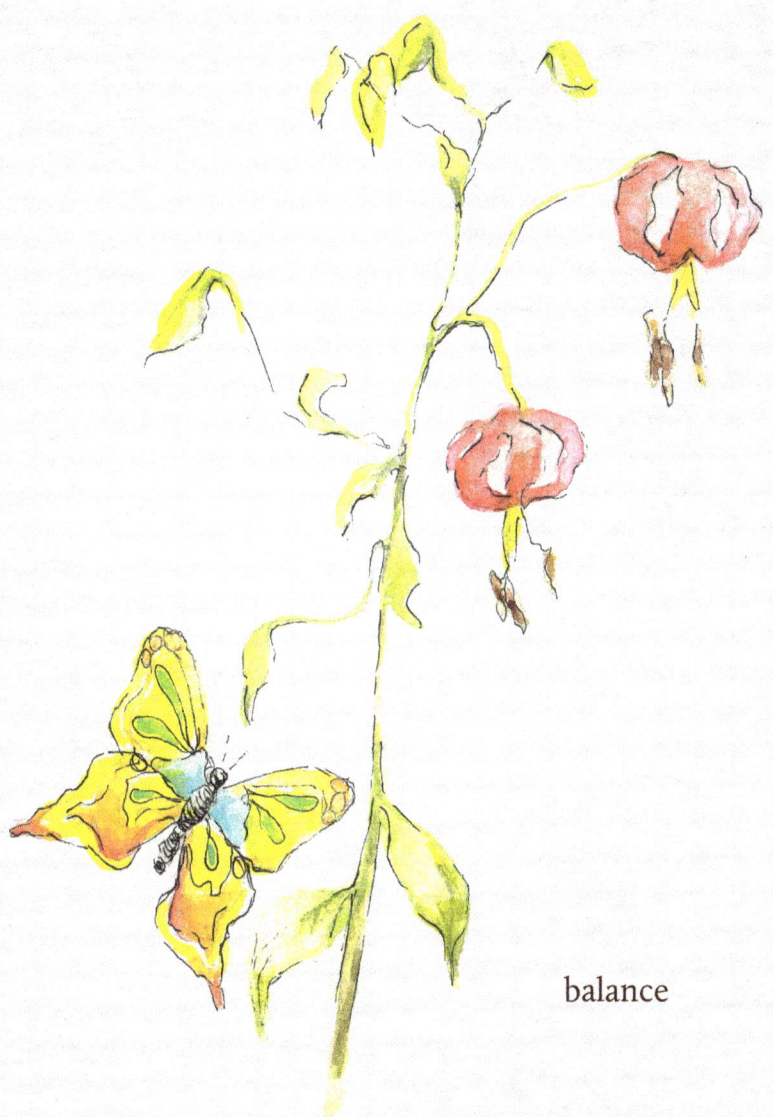

balance

Barbizon school

an art movement originating in the mid-1800s near the village of Barbizon, France, about 30 miles south of Paris. The style represented a shift away from romanticism toward realism. Many paintings of this movement came from trips to the nearby Forest of Fontainebleau where the variety of trees, rocks and landscape encouraged direct observation of nature for artistic inspiration. Influential painters of the Barbizon school included the French Charles-François Daubigny and Theodore Rousseau.

baroque

an important style and period of art, music and architecture during the 1600s and 1700s. The baroque style was strongly supported by the Catholic Church which used the art to promote its religion. Art of this period is dramatic, emotional and uses strong contrasting light and dark colors. Some of the most important baroque artists were the Dutch painters Rembrandt and Vermeer, and the Flemish (from Flanders, a Dutch-speaking area of what is now Belgium) painter Rubens.

bas relief (BAH ruh LEEF)

also *low relief*

See *relief sculpture.*

batik

an art form that originated in Indonesia, it is a technique of dyeing cloth after drawing a design on it with wax. The wax resists the dye, and when removed, reveals the design where the dye did not penetrate the cloth. This process can be repeated several times with intricate designs and many colors.

Bauhaus

a famous art school in Germany that operated from 1919 to 1933. The aim of this school was to bring art back into contact with everyday life and common use. Tying together all the arts and architecture, the school and its philosophy began a movement where communities of artists worked together and learned from each other through experimentation rather than by direct instruction. Many famous artists were influenced by this German art school. Two of the most important Bauhaus artists were the architect Walter Gropius, the school's founder, and the painter Paul Klee.

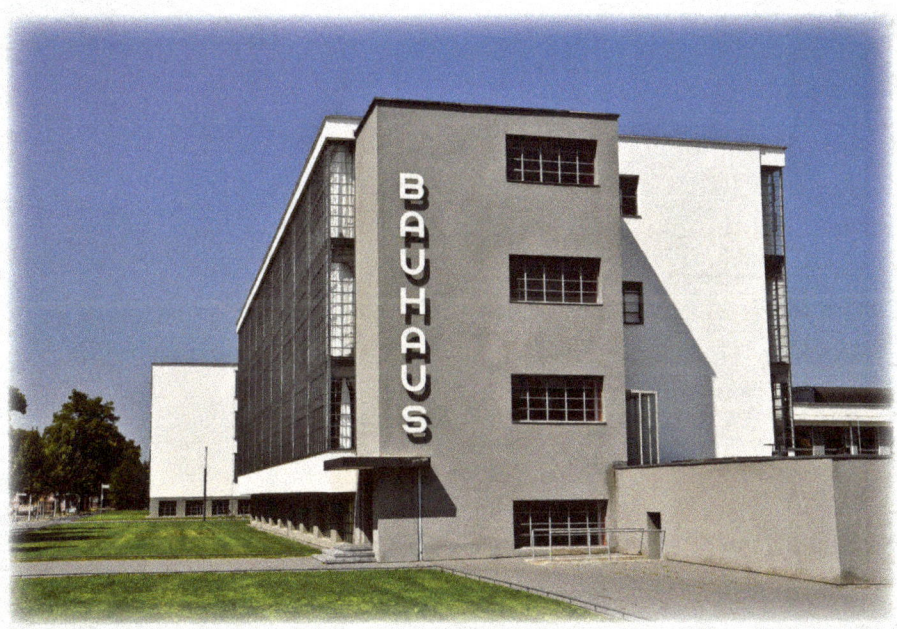

beadwork

beads are small, usually round, pieces of plastic, metal or glass. Beadwork is an art form, or craft, in which beads are threaded together or sewn to fabric to create jewelry, clothing, wall hangings or sculpture.

biennial exhibition
also *biennial*

a large, international art exhibition which takes place every two years. The oldest and most recognized art biennial in the world is the Venice Biennial (*La Biennale di Venezia*) which first opened its doors in 1895.

bird's-eye view

or *aerial view*

a view from above, whether directly or from an angle. If one were to draw or paint a small town as if from the viewpoint of a bird flying a short distance above the town, this would be a bird's-eye or aerial view.

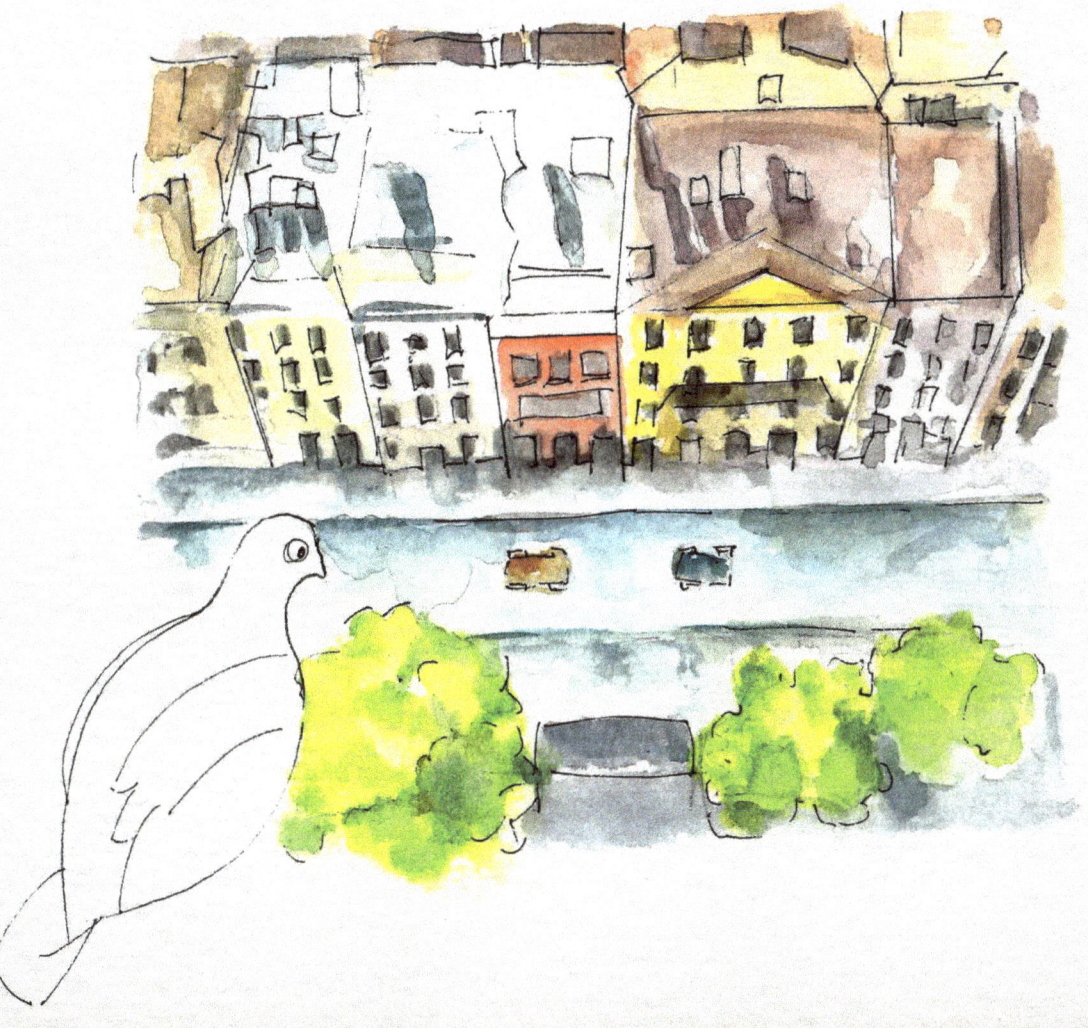

bisque (bisk)

pottery needs to be fired (baked) twice in a kiln. The first firing of a piece of ceramics is called the bisque or *bisque firing*. After the bisque, the piece can be glazed (painted) and then fired again to fix the glaze to the piece.

bleed

allowing one paint color to flow into another color, particularly when both are wet and therefore mix together to some degree. In watercolor painting particularly, there are techniques to both cause and prevent bleeding, depending on the effect desired.

In printmaking, bleed refers to printing right up to the edge. Because it is difficult to print all the way to the edge of a paper or other surface, one prints beyond the intended size, then cuts off the extra. Bleed is the part of the print that is cut off so that the final piece has printing all the way to its edge.

blind contour drawing

a drawing made of the contours of an object without looking at the paper while drawing. One follows the object's outline slowly with their eyes while trying to follow along with their hand. (See *contour* and *contour drawing*.)

blocking in

this is one of the first steps in drawing or painting. The artist makes rough outlines and geometric shapes of their subject in order to see how all the pieces relate to each other and how they fit together on the paper or canvas. After blocking in, the artist can begin to fill in more detailed shapes.

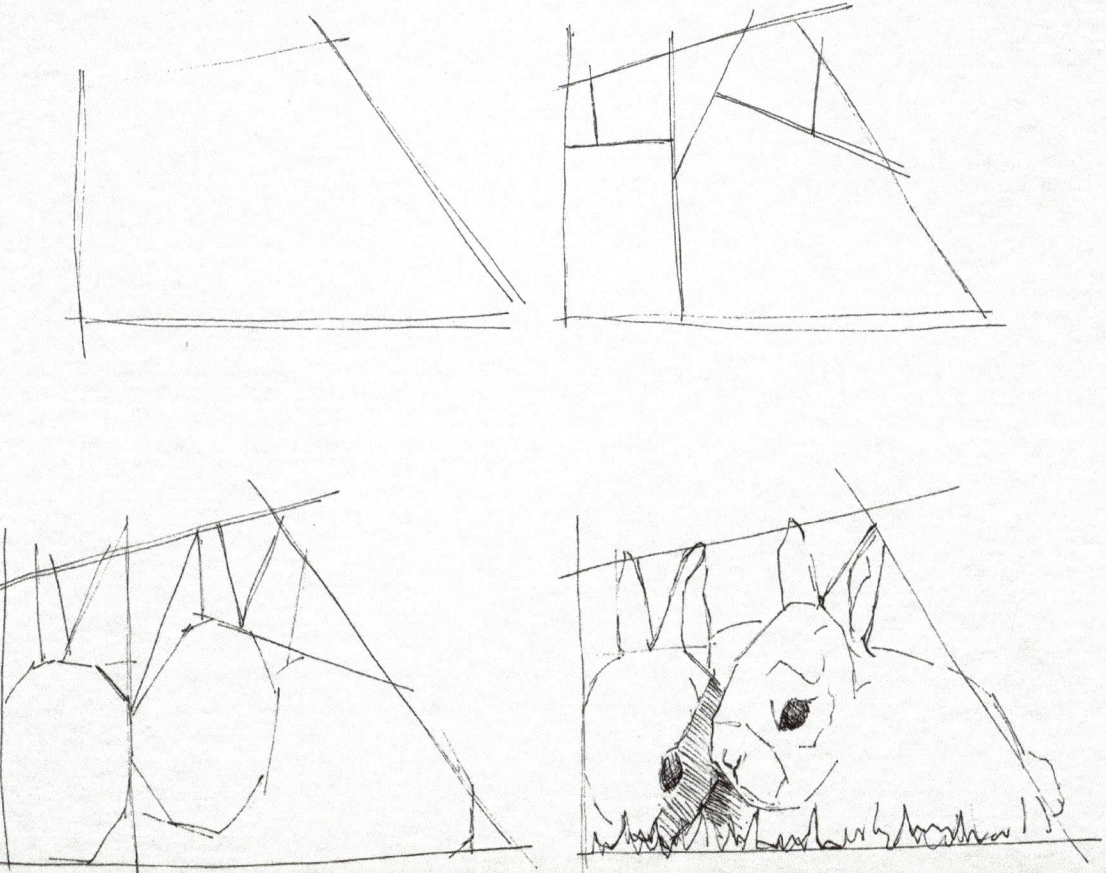

bone dry

the stage in the creation of a ceramic piece when it has air dried as much as possible before being fired for the first time in the kiln.

brayer

a printmaking tool with a handle attached to a roller. It is traditionally used for spreading ink evenly on an area such as an engraved plate or woodcut before pressing it to paper to make a print.

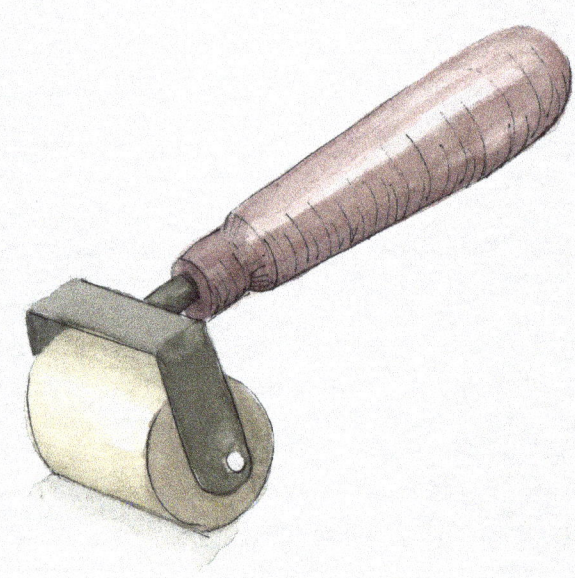

brush

a tool for painting made of natural or synthetic bristles set into a handle. There are hundreds of different sizes, shapes and types of brushes designed for different specialized uses.

brush stroke

the movement made by a brush in painting or the resulting look and texture on the canvas or paper, which varies according to the pressure, movement and amount of paint applied.

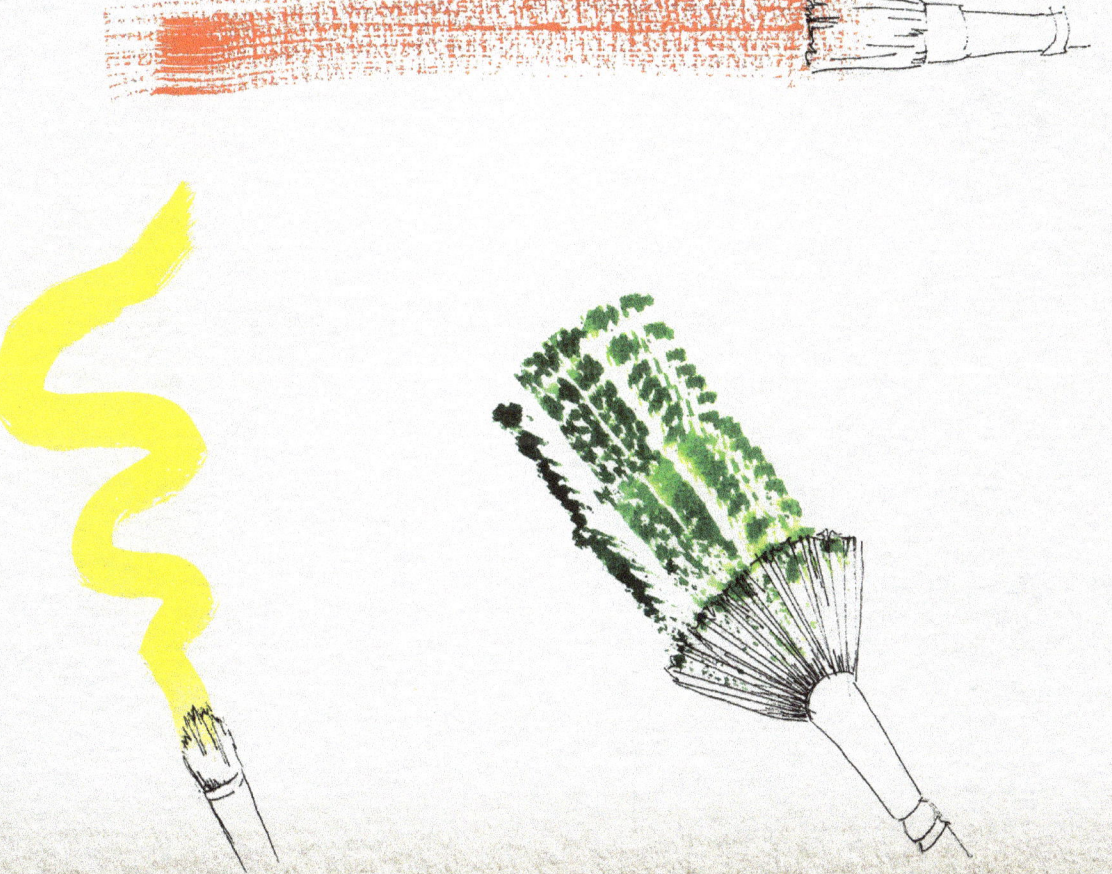

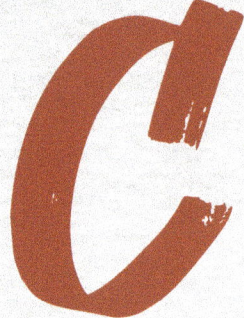

calligraphy

the art of beautiful writing or lettering.

Calligraphy

canvas

a strong fabric normally stretched around a wooden frame as a surface to paint on. The most commonly used fabrics are cotton or linen, the latter being regarded as the finest choice.

caricature

a drawing or painting of a person or thing in which the features have been exaggerated or changed to make the image funny, silly or ridiculous.

carve

to cut out sections or pieces of a material to create a sculpture.

cast

to create a sculpture of metal or other material by pouring it in liquid form into a mold, then removing the mold when the material has hardened.

cast shadow

See *shadow and light types.*

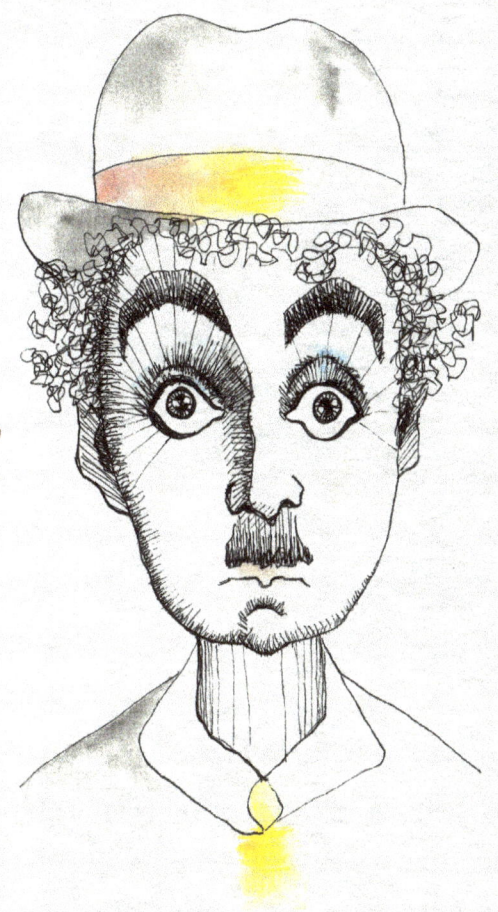

center axis

an axis, or center axis, is an imaginary line running through the center of an object or shape. Also called *tilt lines*, they can be used to identify inclinations, proportions or balances of objects in drawing.

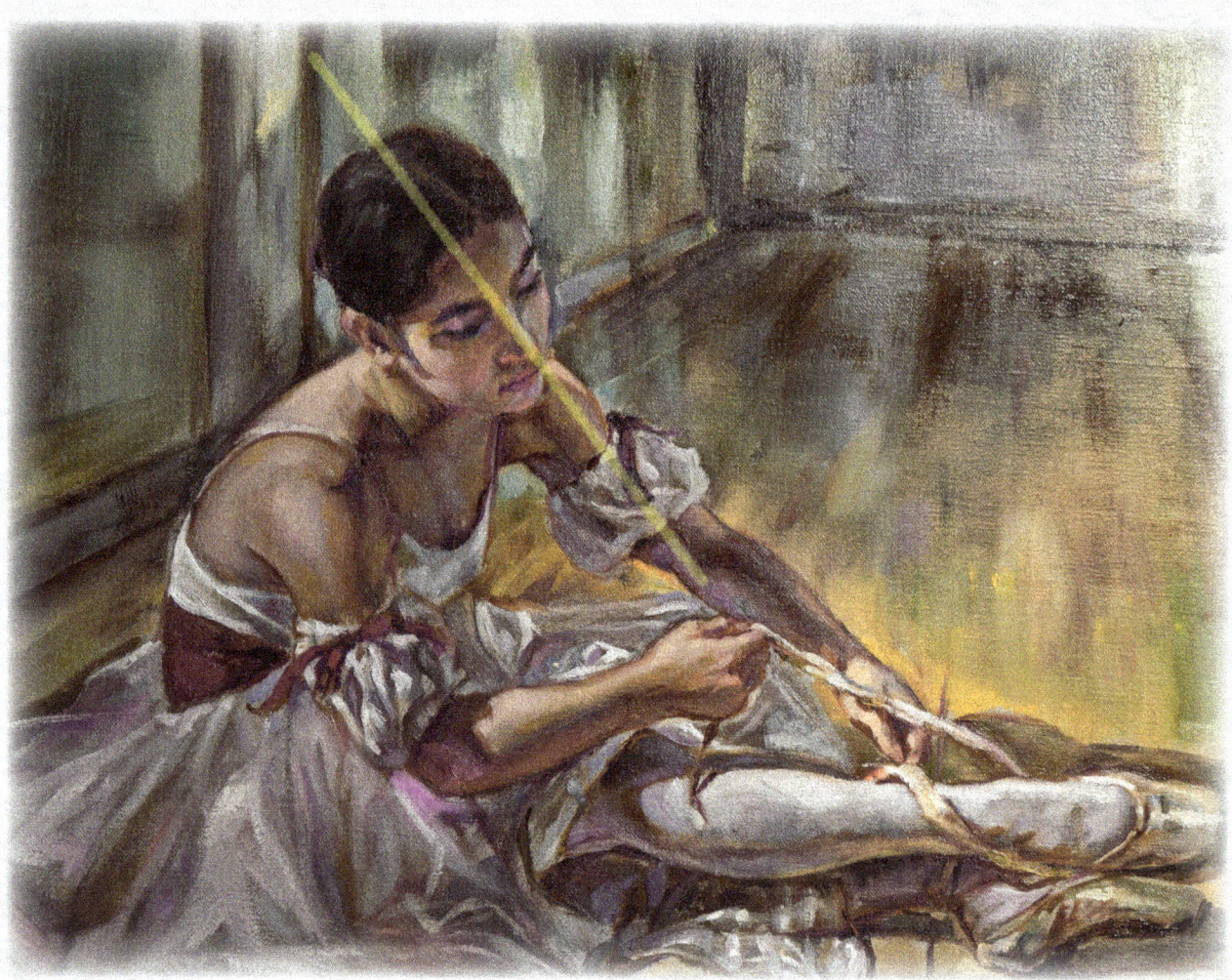

ceramics

the general term used for art made with clay and then fired to enhance its hardness and durability.

charcoal

a black, crumbly carbon substance (the result of burning wood slowly) from which charcoal drawing pencils, crayons or sticks are made. It smudges easily and creates softer, thicker lines than most other drawing substances. It is frequently used for quick sketches but can also be used for completed drawings, in which case it has to be sprayed with a fixative so that it doesn't smear.

chiaroscuro (kee AHR oh SKYOO roh)

the use of strongly contrasting lights and darks in painting and drawing. From Italian *chiaro*, "clear" or "light" + *oscuro*, "obscure" or "dark."

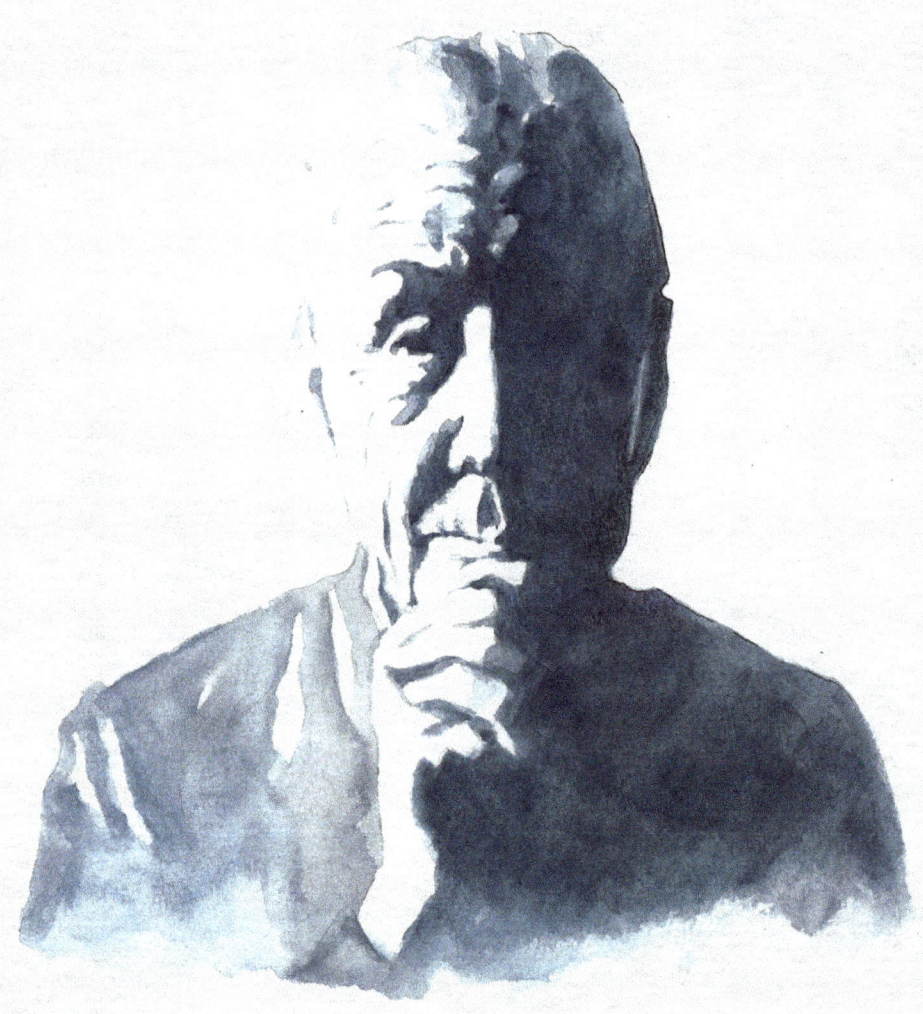

chisel

a metal instrument with a slanted edge used for carving sculptures of stone, wood, or other material.

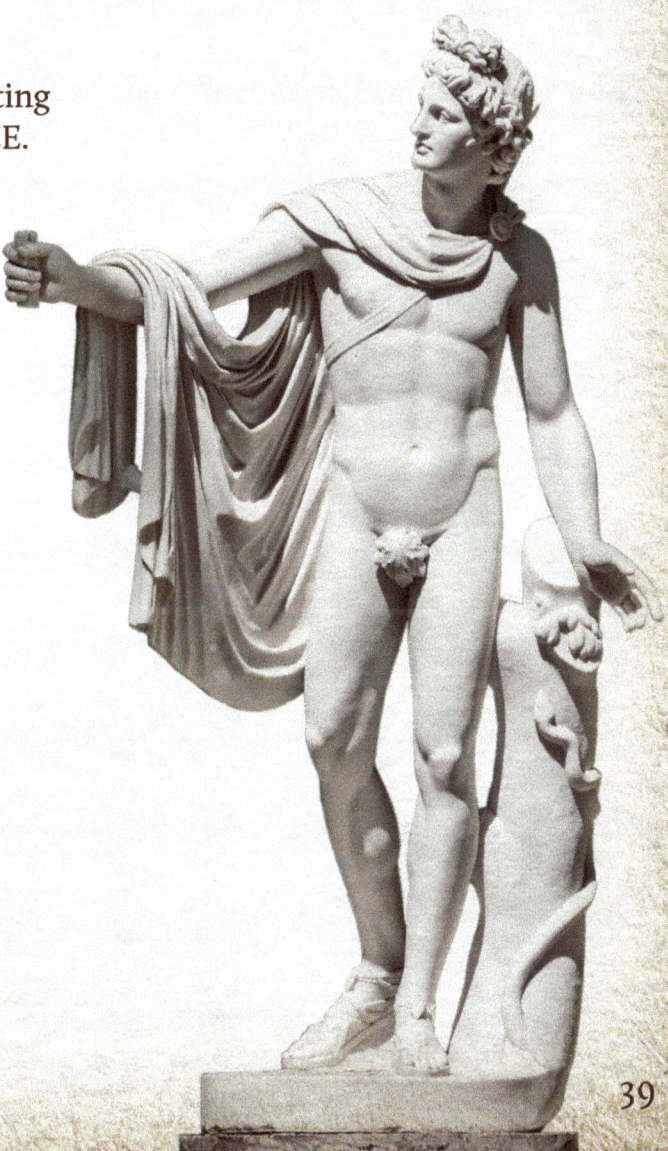

classical art

also *classicism*

art of Ancient Greece and Rome, dating from about 500 BCE to about 400 CE. Art of this period idealized the human figure and valued a harmony and balance of form. Appreciation of classical art, its forms and methods, was renewed a thousand years later in the Renaissance. (See *ancient art.*)

clay

a specific kind of heavy, wet earth that is soft and moldable but when fully dried through baking becomes very hard. It can then be covered with a glaze to create permanent, beautiful works of art and pottery.

collage art

art that is made by gluing things together. Collage can be made with paper, cloth, objects or anything else glued or stuck together. From French *coller*, "to glue."

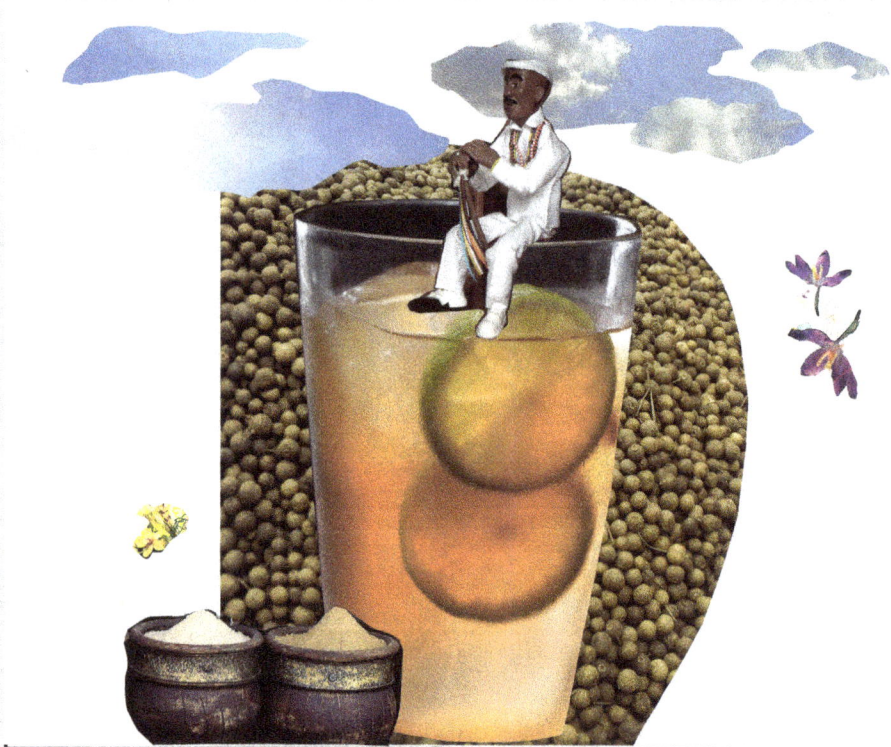

color

a visual perception of red, green, blue, etc., resulting from different wavelengths of light. As light hits an object, some wavelengths (colors) are absorbed by the object and others bounce off. What we perceive as color are the wavelengths of light that bounce off the object into the eye.

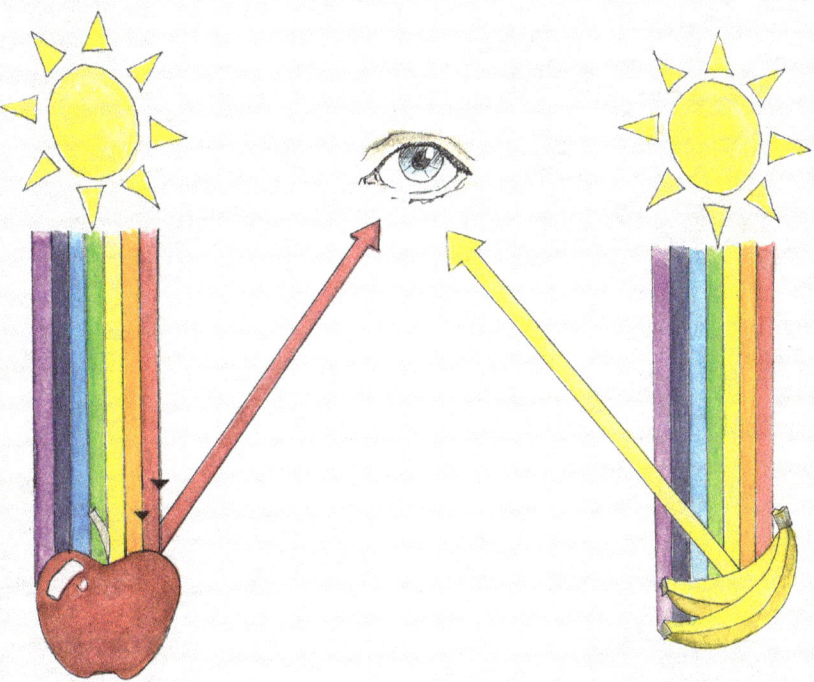

Of the different colors, red has the longest wavelength, progressing through orange, yellow, green and blue to violet, which has the shortest wavelength. A rainbow is an example of light being broken down into its component colors.

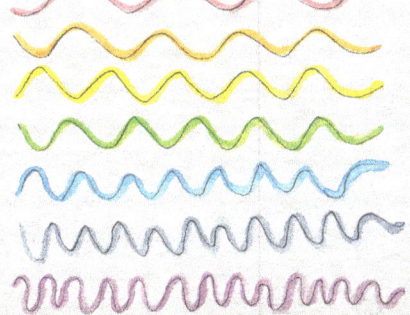

color value

color value refers to how dark or how light a color is. A color value can be darkened by adding its complementary color or black. It can be lightened by adding white or sometimes a lighter color such as yellow. In watercolor, a color can be lightened by adding more water.

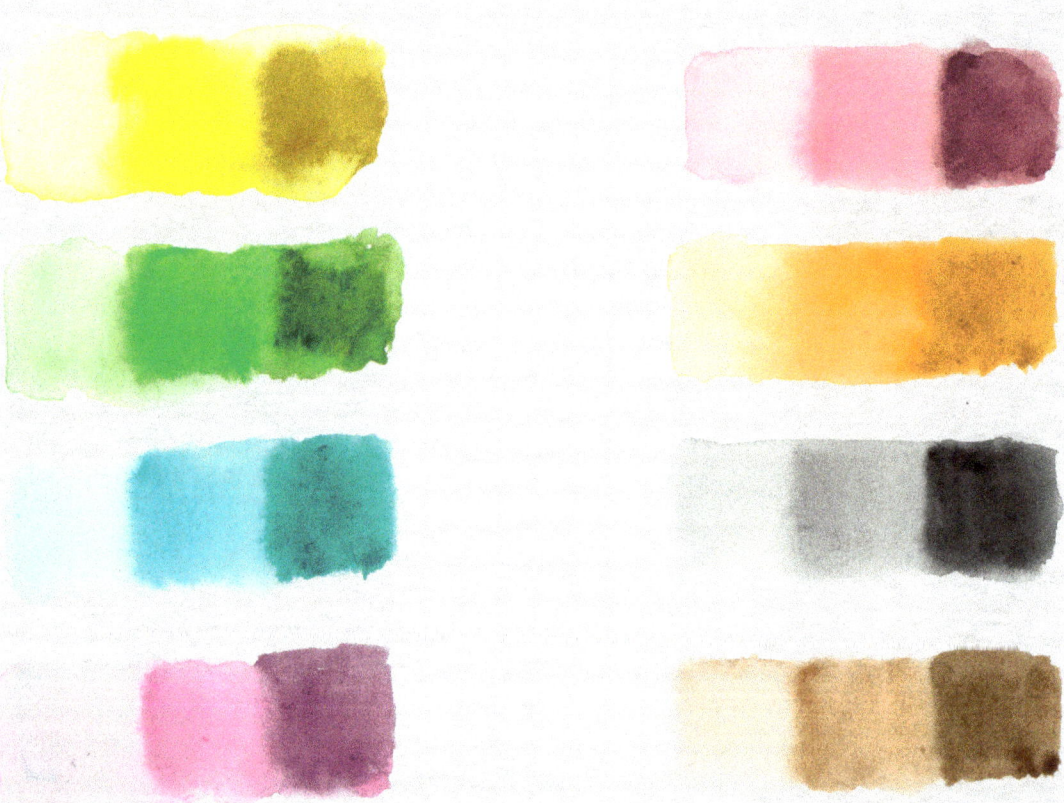

color wheel

a circle around which colors are arranged according to their wavelengths (see *color*) to show relationships between them. It is a tool to help artists understand and combine colors with greater precision.

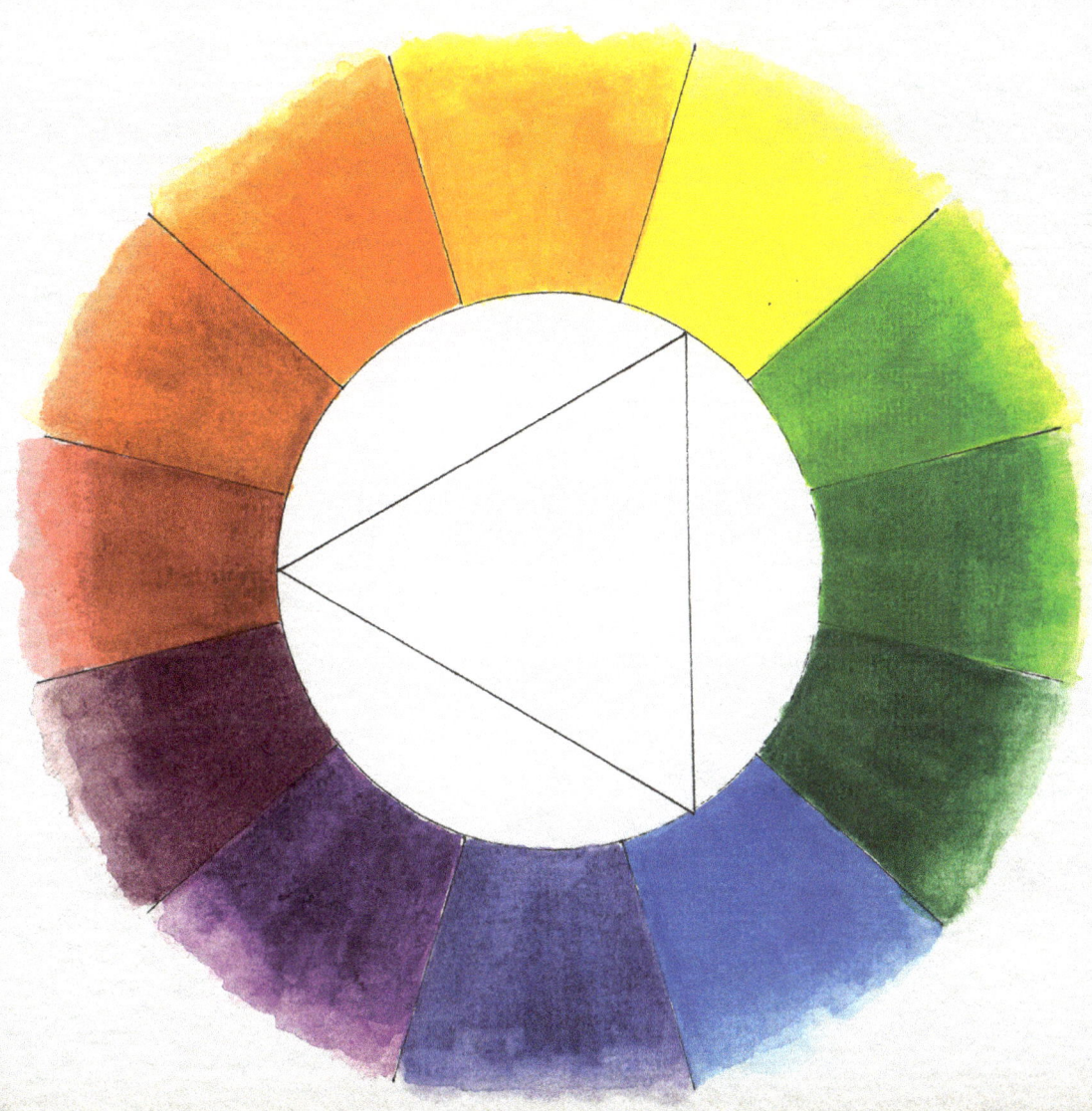

complement

to make something better or complete by the addition of something else. For example, you might say, "That hat complements your outfit perfectly!"

complementary colors

pairs of colors that contrast with each other. Complementary colors are directly opposite each other on a color wheel. When used side-by-side or near one another, they stand out or seem brighter. A color can also be darkened by adding some of its complementary color. Examples of complementary colors are blue and orange, red and green, yellow and violet. (Compare *analogous colors*.)

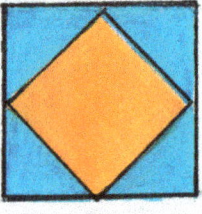
orange & blue

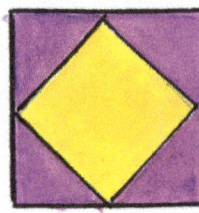
yellow & violet

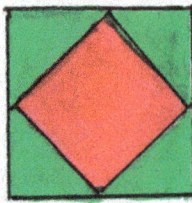
red & green

composition

the arrangement of the different parts or elements of a painting or visual work of art to create a pleasing design.

computer art

also *digital art*

art that is partly or completely generated on a computer or other digital device.

conceptual art

an art movement started in the 1960s, but inspired by earlier movements, in which the idea or concept of the artist became more important than the actual finished work of art, such as a painting or sculpture. Conceptual art can be almost anything the artist decides conveys a concept, from a simple object to flashing lights, a poem, or a performance. It is art focused on ideas rather than objects. Two of the most well-known conceptual artists of that time were the Americans Solomon "Sol" LeWitt and Joseph Kosuth; however, many conceptual artists continue the movement, including the Chinese artist Ai Weiwei and the Japanese-American artist Yoko Ono.

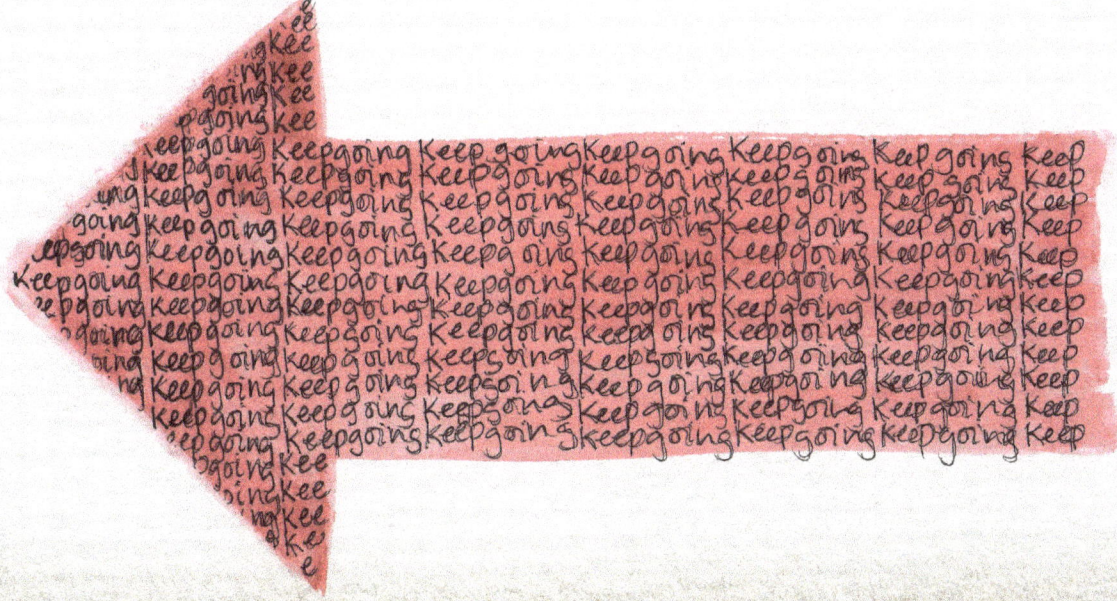

cone

also *pyrometric cone*

small pyramid-shaped objects placed in a kiln to measure the heat (*pyro-*, "fire" + *metric*, "measure"). Cones are numbered according to the time and temperature required for them to melt. By observing a cone, one can tell when the ceramic pieces being fired should be done.

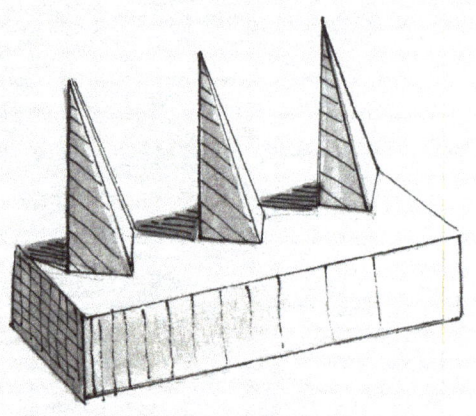 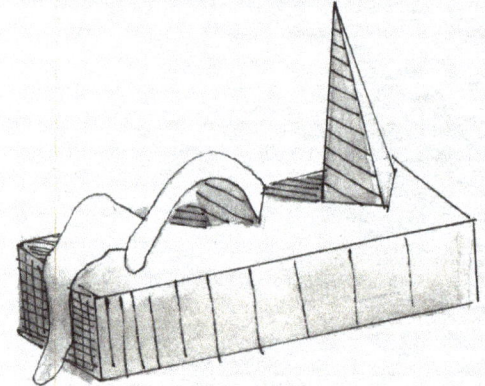

contemporary art

a general term for art of today or the recent past, often referring to art after World War II or from the mid-1960s to present day.
(Compare *modern art*.)

contour

also *contours*

the outline or outside edges of a shape or form. From French *contour,* "edge."

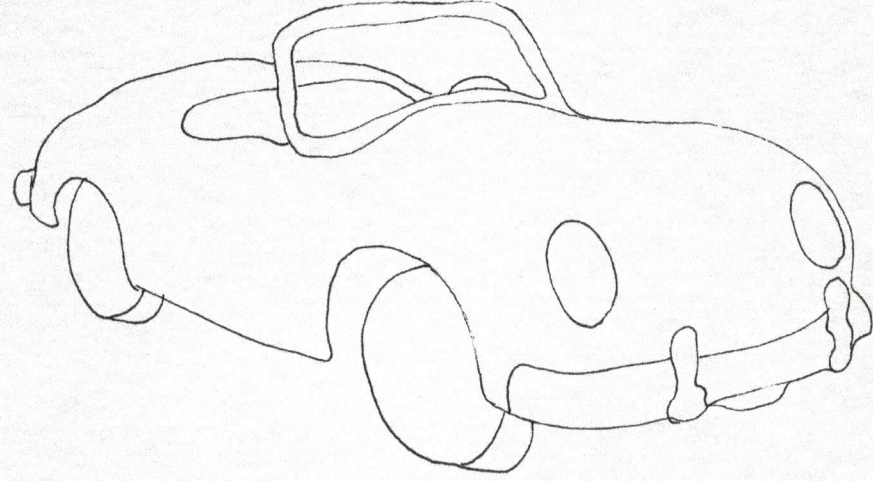

contour drawing

a drawing of the outline or contours of an object, making longer lines that flow rather than small, choppy lines. (Compare *blind contour drawing.*)

contrast

a noticeable difference between things. In visual art, contrast can be shown through shapes, colors, directions, sizes or other elements, but most often it refers to differences in value. The greatest contrast in value is of course between black and white. This is called *high contrast*.

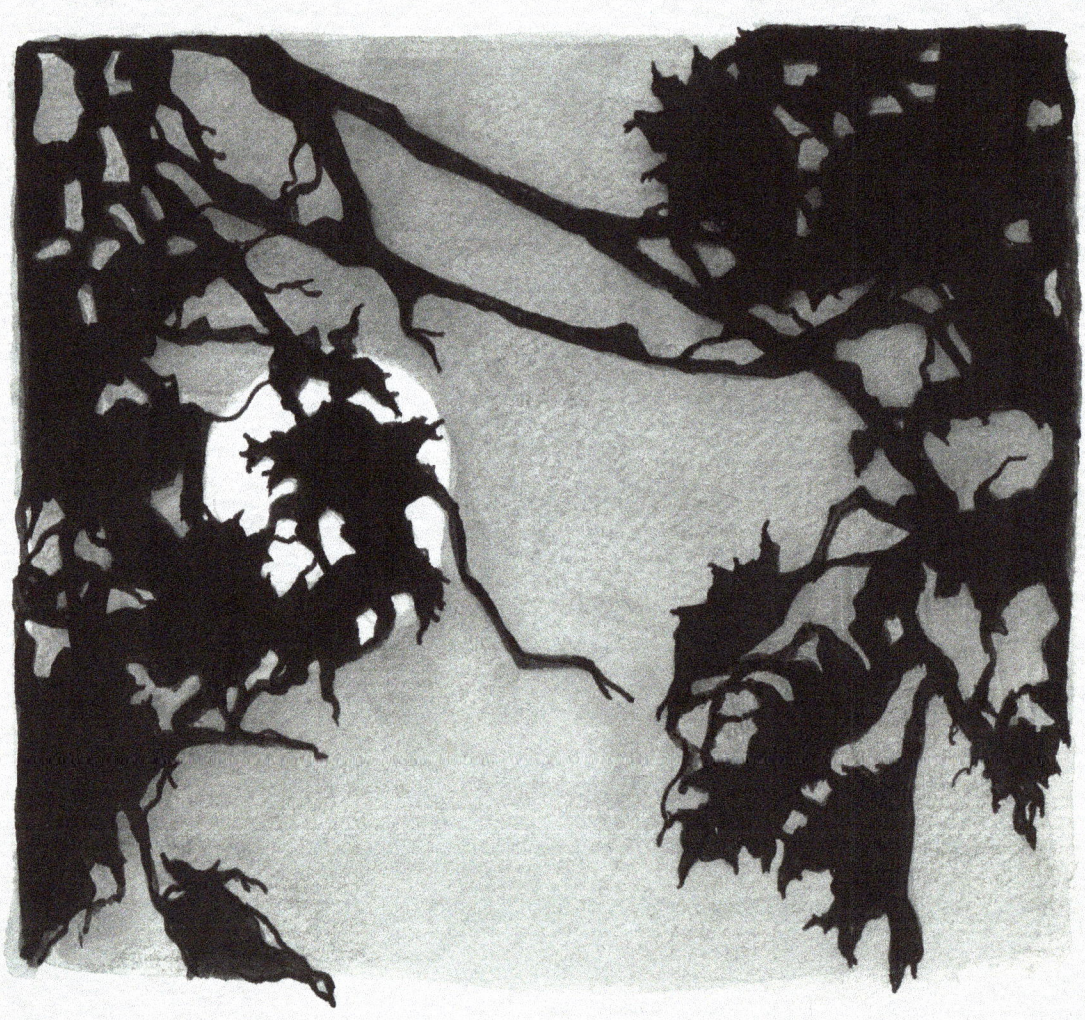

contrasting colors

another word for *complementary colors*, though the term contrasting colors is often used in a more general way to describe colors that may not be exactly opposite each other on a color wheel. Like complementary colors, contrasting colors placed next to each other will tend to stand out or look brighter.

cool

colors that tend to have blue in them are often called cool. This comes from the observation that objects in nature that are cold or cool, like ice, tend to look blue. (Compare *warm*.)

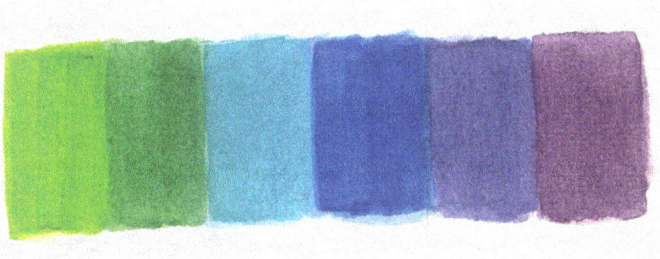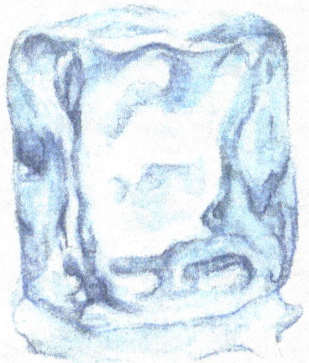

core light

also *direct light*

See *shadow and light types*.

core shadow

See *shadow and light types*.

crafts

a general term referring to the making of things by hand, usually things that have some practical use such as for eating, drinking or wearing. Crafts, though often very creative and artistic, are normally considered different than fine art.

craftsmanship

a word used to describe the quality of something created, usually by hand. It implies that the work was done with skill, care and attention to detail. Also used to describe the skill of the person, such as, "She showed great craftsmanship in her weaving designs."

crash point

See *rule of thirds.*

cross contour lines

in drawing, a way of conveying the form of an object by drawing lines that follow the changes in direction of planes and curves of that object.

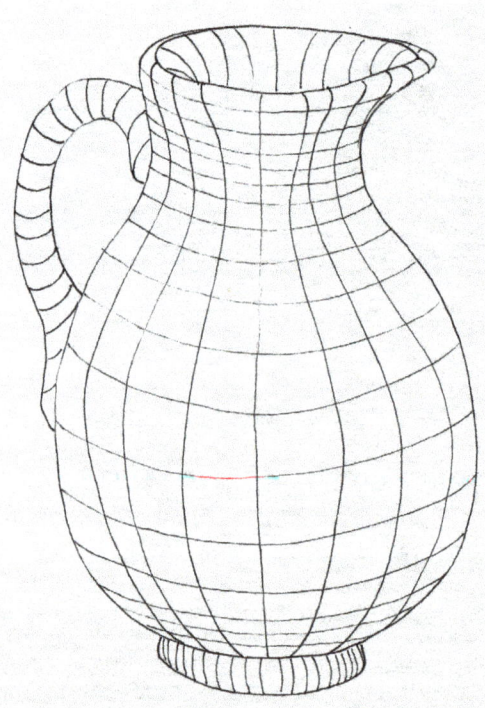

cross hatching

in drawing and engraving, *hatching* is a way of darkening an area by use of parallel lines. The closer together the lines are, the darker the area. Further layers of parallel lines on top of the hatching but going in different directions, called cross hatching, can be used to make the area even darker. This technique is used for creating darker and lighter areas of a drawing, such as showing different degrees of shadow on an apple. From French *hacher,* "to cut up."

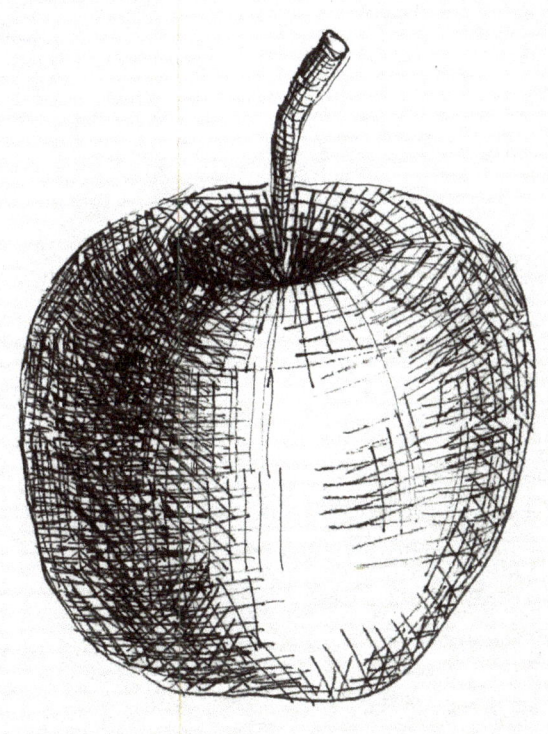

cubism

an art movement originated by the Spanish artist Pablo Picasso and the French artist George Braque in 1907-08. In cubism, artists aimed to show different sides of an object or person at the same time. This was done by dividing the painting into cubes or sections that represented different viewpoints of the same thing. It became one of the most influential styles of the 1900s.

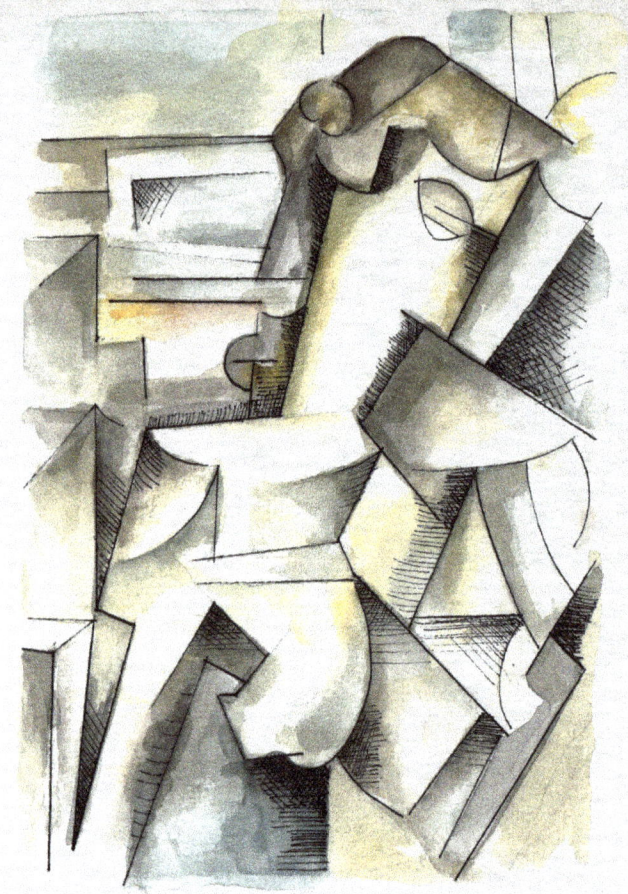

curator

a person hired by a museum or gallery to buy or choose art which they consider to be relevant to that organization's art philosophy and style. A curator also organizes exhibitions of specific artists or groups of artists and decides the arrangement of the artwork throughout the museum or gallery. From Latin *curare*, "take care of."

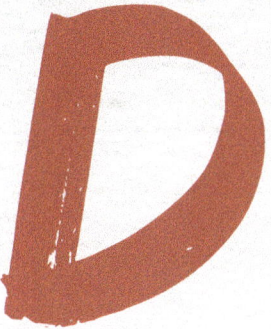

decorative arts

arts or crafts with the purpose of creating objects that have a practical use but are also beautiful, such as pottery, clothing and furniture. In cultures of the Far East and Middle East, there was no traditional distinction between the fine arts and decorative arts because most pieces considered "art" were also functional; for example, a finely crafted and decorated Chinese tea service or an elaborately designed Persian rug.

decoupage

the art of decorating an object by cutting out images or patterns from paper or fabric and gluing them onto the object. It can include adding ink, paint or other material as well. Traditionally, a decoupaged object is covered with many layers of clear glue and sanded so the additions appear to be part of the object, not stuck on it. Common objects for decoupaging include boxes, frames, ceramic pieces, shelves and parts of furniture. From French *decouper,* "to cut out."

design

the arrangement of colors, lines, shapes or light.

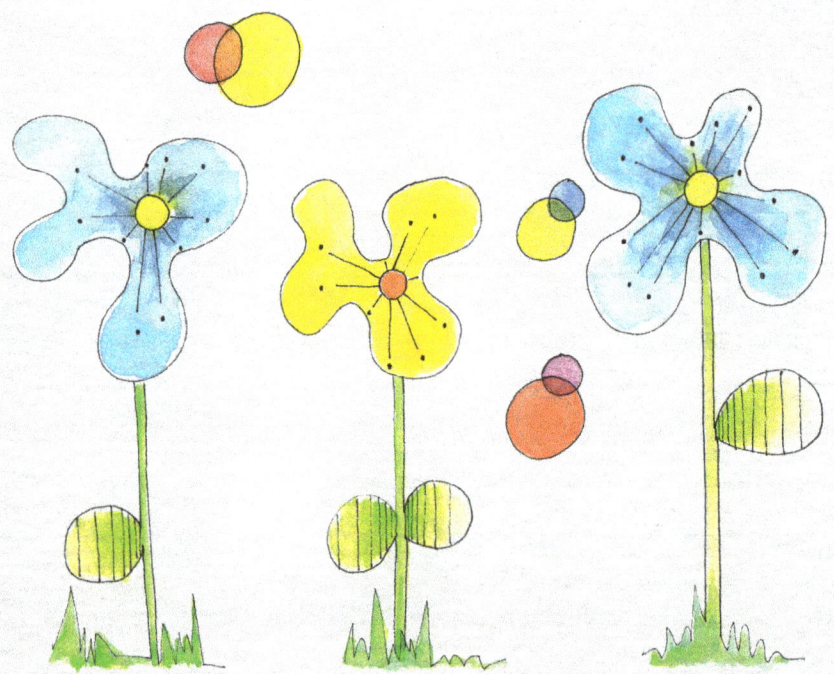

digital art

or *computer art*

art that is partly or completely generated on a computer or other digital device.

diptych (dip tick)

originally, a work made of two painted or carved panels hinged together. Now, diptych can refer to any set of two art pieces (such as paintings, photographs or literary works) that are meant to go together. From Greek *di-,* "two" + *ptukhe,* "to fold."

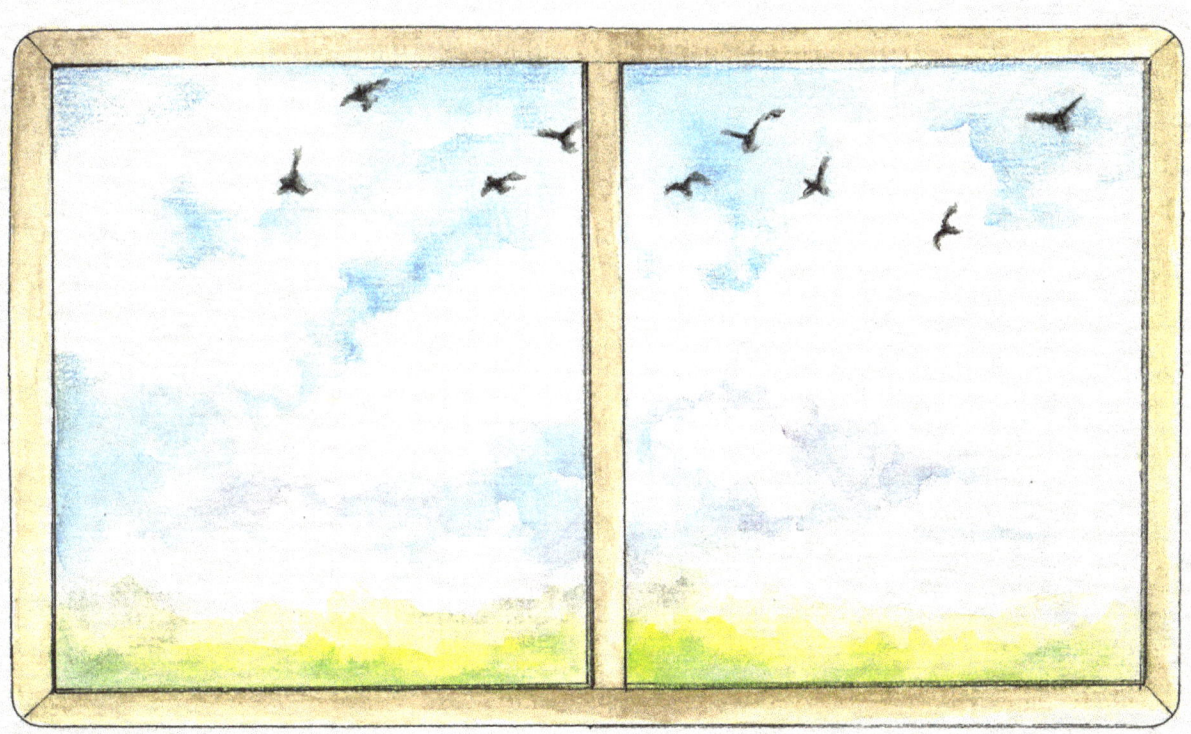

direct light

also *core light*

See *shadow and light types.*

documentary

a movie or video using footage of real people and events, and covering some historical, political or social topic in an informative way. Documentaries are frequently used for educational purposes.

drawing

an art technique in which an image is created using lines and shading. Drawings are usually done with pencil, crayon, charcoal or ink.

drawing pencils

graphite pencils used for drawing. They are categorized as H (hard) or B (soft). Hard pencils leave thin, light lines. Soft pencils leave broad, dark marks that are easier to smear. The higher the number, the harder (H) or softer (B) the graphite—see diagram.

Pencils in between hard and soft are labeled HB or F (sharpens to a fine point). The H and B come from the French *haut,* "high" and *bas,* "low" in reference to the amount of hardening material added to the graphite.

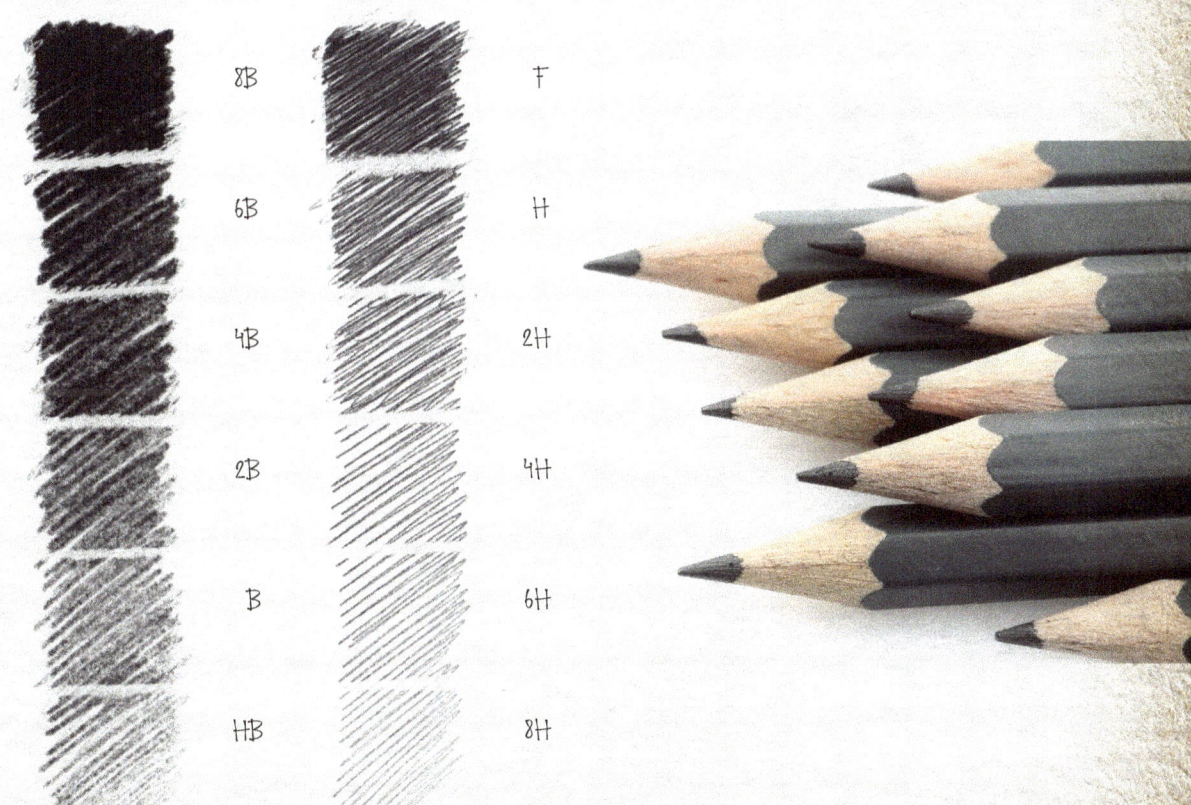

dry mount

a process by which photographs or art prints are permanently mounted to a foam board or other surface using a thin sheet of heat-activated adhesive. This helps keep the piece in place and prevents wrinkling or creasing.

drypoint

a method of printmaking in which the artist draws with a very sharp, needle-like instrument on a metal plate, frequently copper. The plate is inked, then wiped off, so that ink remains only in the grooves. A sheet of paper is pressed to the plate, transferring the image to the paper.

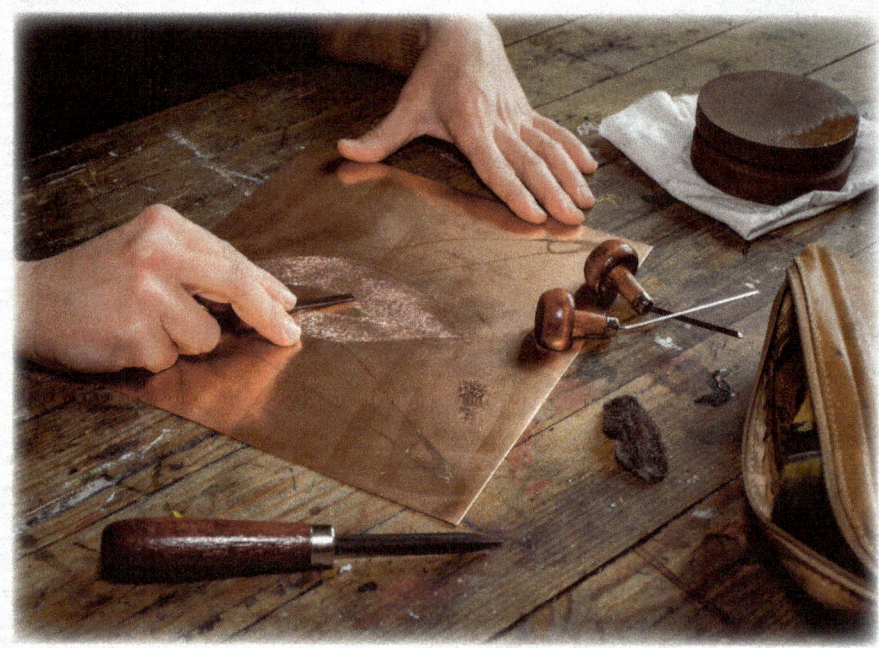

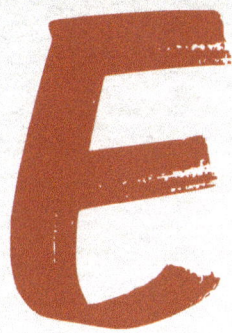

earth tones

or *earth colors*

this term has various meanings, but most commonly it refers to colors that have some brown, the color of soil or "earth." The term can also be used to include grays, greens and even reds commonly found in nature, particularly when they are somewhat subdued, not pure or bright.

earthenware

pottery that retains some water-absorption quality and is rougher to the touch. To be used for holding liquids, or for decorative purposes, it can be glazed.

easel

an upright support for holding a canvas or other surface while an artist works on it.

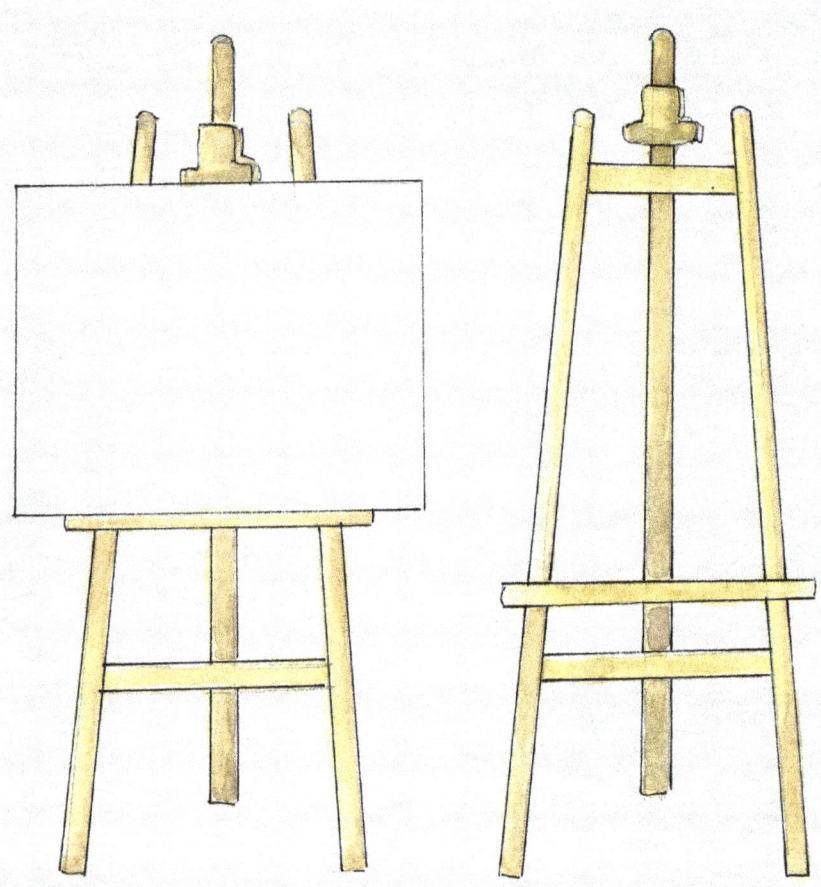

edition

in certain art forms, the original artwork is reproduced into multiple copies by the artist. For example, the artist makes a single etching, drawing or engraving either on a metal plate, a stone or on wood; this original work is called the *master*. From that master many copies can be made, all of which are thought of as a set of essentially identical works. The whole set is called an edition, though the term can also refer to a single one of these prints. In most cases, all the copies of a single edition are numbered and signed by the artist. When only a certain number of copies will be made and no more, it is called a *limited edition*. Editions can also exist for sculptures, video, photography or digital art.

enamel

a hard, shiny glaze made of powdered glass used to decorate metal, glass or ceramics. It is applied to the surface of an object and baked at a high temperature, which fuses (combines into one) the glaze to the surface, resulting in a smooth, glossy finish.

engraving

a method of printmaking. It is done by drawing with a sharp tool on wood or metal, then applying ink to the scratched (engraved) surface and wiping off the excess so it remains in the engraved parts only. A print is made by pressing paper to the surface, so the inked portions transfer to the paper. Many images can be made from one engraving.

environmental art

or nature art or land art

art that is done in the natural environment using elements of nature, such as rocks, leaves, twigs or snow. Environmental art is often designed to last for a short time and then decompose back to nature. It often includes a message or purpose designed to support or protect the natural environment. The resulting art piece can be photographed for broader distribution. Well-known environmental artists include American artist Andy Goldsworthy, German artist Nils-Udo and the Bulgarian artist Christo and his Moroccan marital and artistic partner Jeanne-Claude.

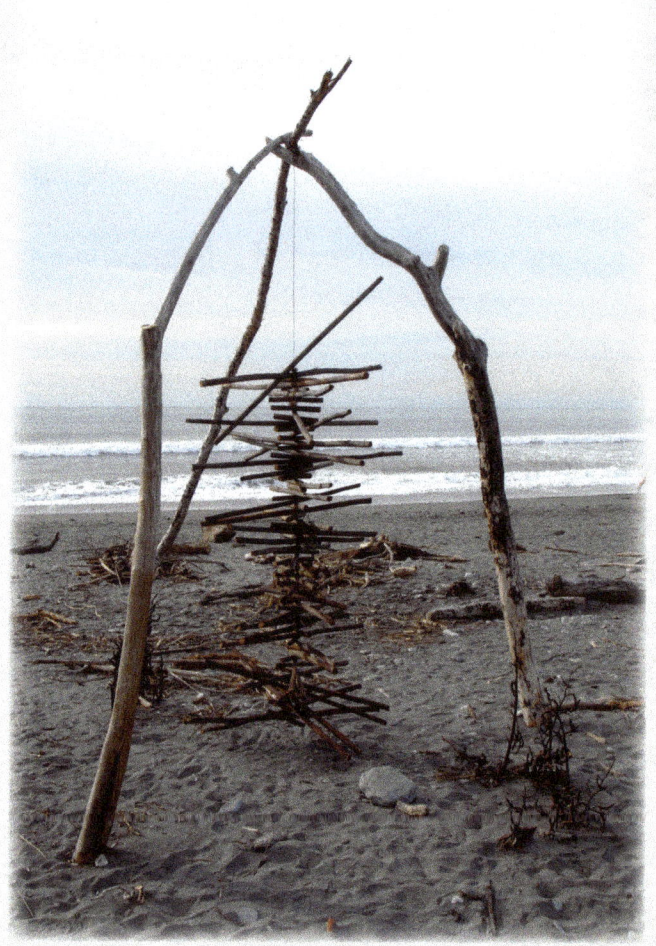

ephemeral art

ephemeral means "lasting only a short time." It comes from Greek *ephemeros,* "lasting only a day." Ephemeral art is meant to last for only a short period of time. It might be a performance that is done only once, a sculpture made of food which will decompose, or a projection of color on a wall.

eraser

a tool for getting rid of previously drawn lines. Some erasers are very soft and are used to clean up general areas of a drawing while others are hard and can be used to erase very precise areas.

etching

a printing method in which an artist draws on a metal plate coated with an acid-resistant material. The artist's lines expose the metal by scraping off this coating. The metal plate is immersed in an acid which eats away the exposed metal lines, producing deep grooves. The plate can be inked and used to make copies of the drawing. This is different from drypoint, which does not use acid to create the grooves. (Compare *drypoint.*)

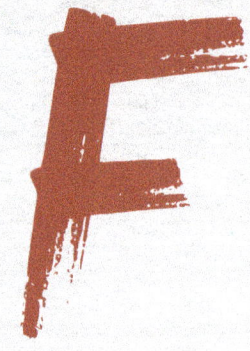

F

a label on a pencil showing that the lead is of medium softness-hardness and can be sharpened to a fine point. (See *drawing pencils.*)

Fauvism

a brief art movement in the early 1900s characterized by the use of bright, intense colors, simplified forms, and strong, somewhat wild brush strokes. The leaders of this movement were the French painters André Derain and Henri Matisse. The name Fauvism came from a critic who called their paintings *les Fauves*, French for "the wild beasts." The term was later used to describe the artists themselves.

figurative art

art that seeks to represent objects or people
in a way that they can easily be recognized.
(Compare *abstract art.*)

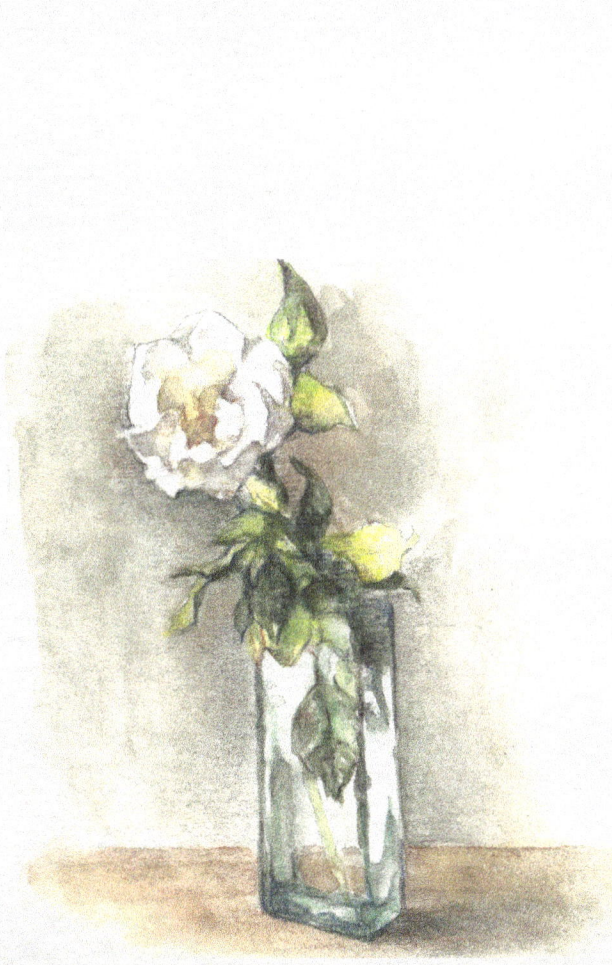

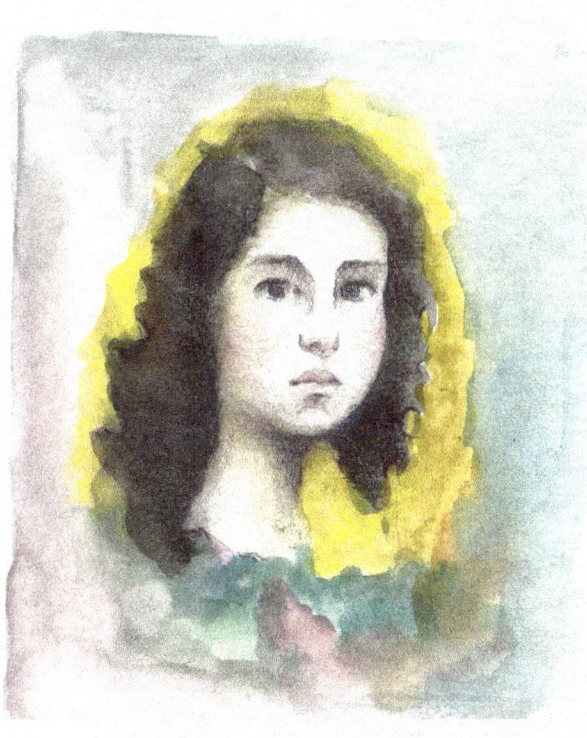

figure drawing

drawing of the human figure in different positions or postures using any of a variety of drawing media, such as pencil, charcoal, pen and ink, etc. When done from an actual model, it is called *life drawing.*

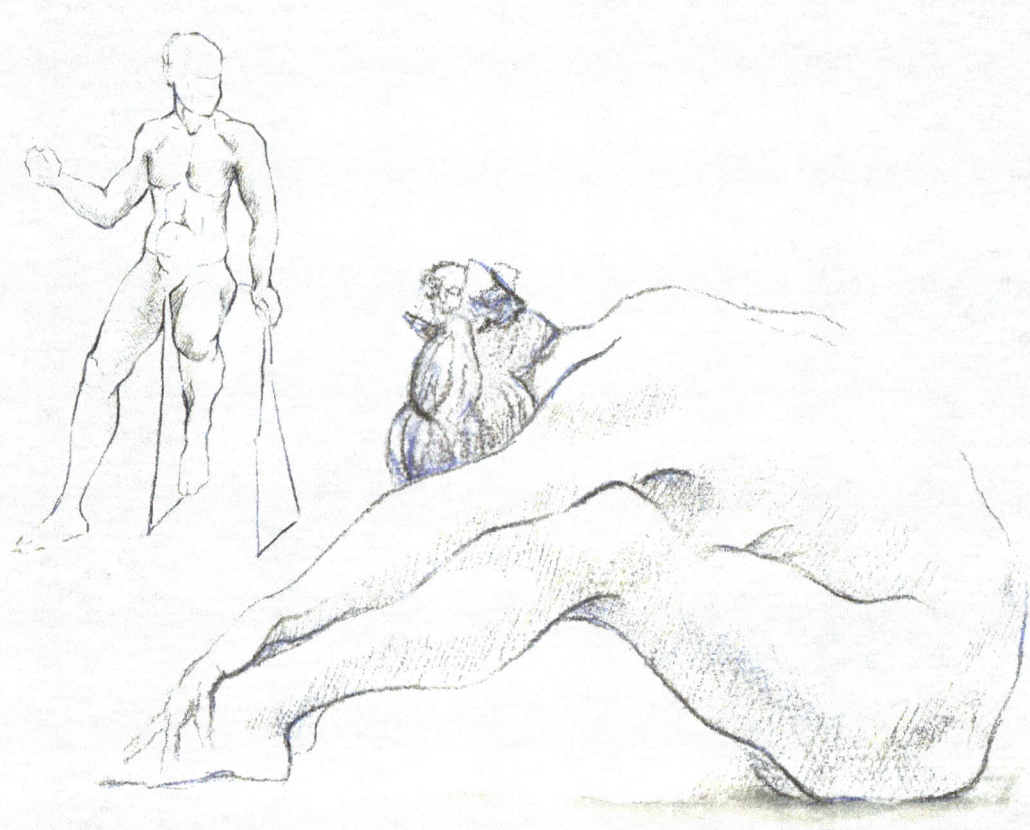

fine art

art which is done for the purpose of aesthetics, or the communication of emotion, concepts or ideas only, in contrast to art that has a practical use. (Compare *crafts.*)

fire

bake a ceramic piece in a kiln in order to dry and harden it or to fuse a glaze to its surface.

fixative

a chemical sprayed onto finished pieces created with media like charcoal, pastel or watercolor to protect them from smearing or fading.

folk art

art that represents the cultural traditions of a group or community, often created with limited tools and for mainly practical purposes. The folk art of a particular group or region is usually characterized by a distinctive style unique to that community, culture or region.

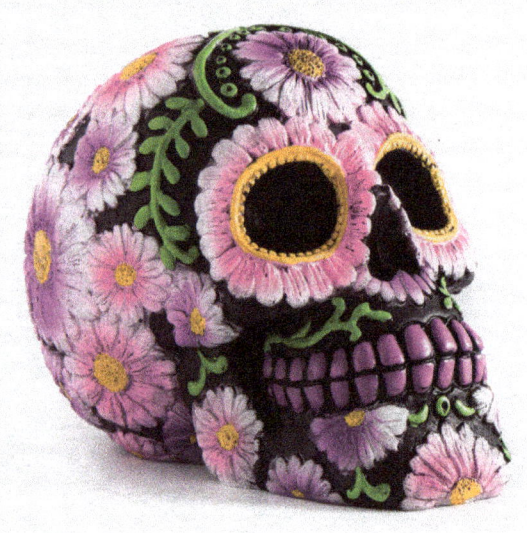

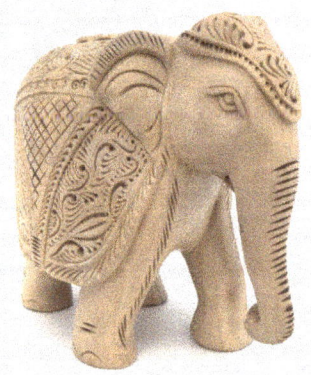

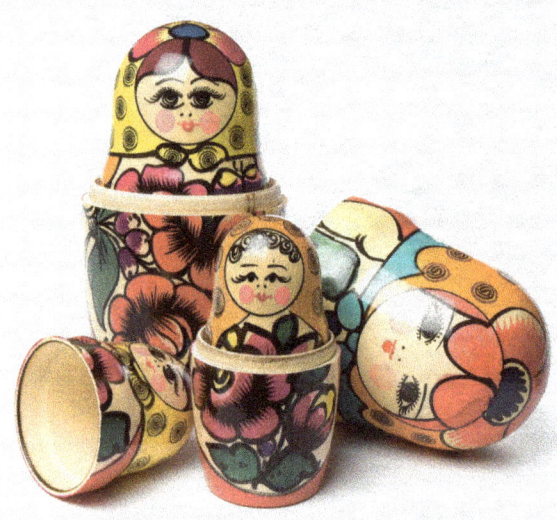

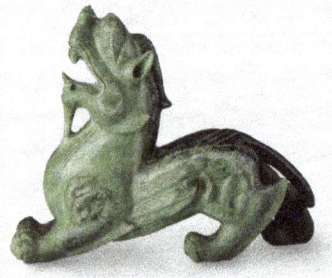

font

a complete set of all characters, including uppercase and lowercase letters, numerals and other symbols, all in a particular style. Different fonts can communicate different moods, concepts and intentions. (See *typography*.)

ABCDEFG
HIJKLMN
OPQRST
UVWXYZ
01234

foreground

the area of a painting that appears to be nearest the viewer. (Compare *background.*)

foreground

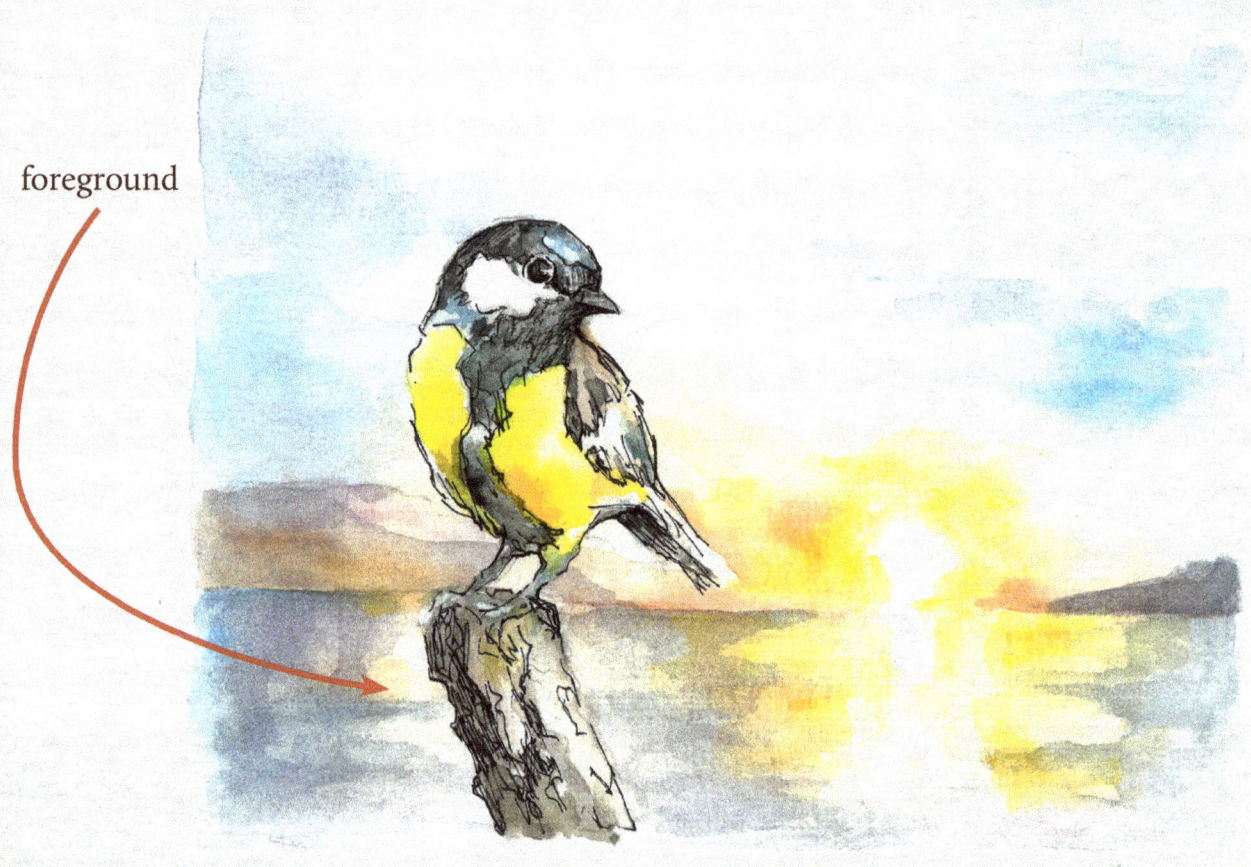

70

foreshortening

a drawing technique that produces the illusion that some part of an object or person is closer to the viewer than another. For example, if you were drawing a girl reaching her open hand toward you, the hand would appear much larger than the face even though in reality it is not.

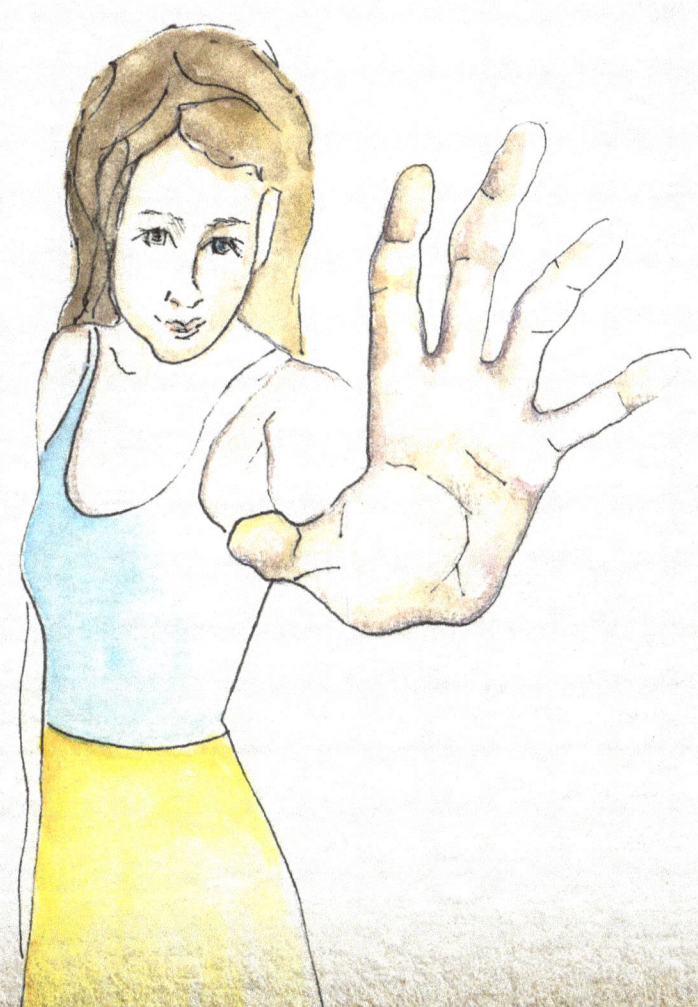

form

a word used for objects that have the three dimensions of length, width and height. All sculptures are considered forms, but even in drawing or painting, an object with the illusion of three dimensions is called a form.

found object art
or *readymade art*

art created from any object which was not originally meant for an artistic purpose but has been reused to create a work of art. As early conceptual art, this art form began in 1917, when the French-American artist Marcel Duchamp bought and signed a urinal and called it art. A famous found object piece called Lobster Telephone was created by surrealist artist Salvador Dalí in 1936.

fresco painting

a technique in which an artist paints directly on a wet plaster wall (or ceiling) with water-based pigments so the painting becomes part of the wall as the plaster dries. Used mainly for mural painting, the process results in a painting that is non-reflective and extremely durable, retaining its beauty for a long time. Many famous paintings from the Renaissance are frescoes, such as those spanning the Sistine Chapel ceiling by Michelangelo.

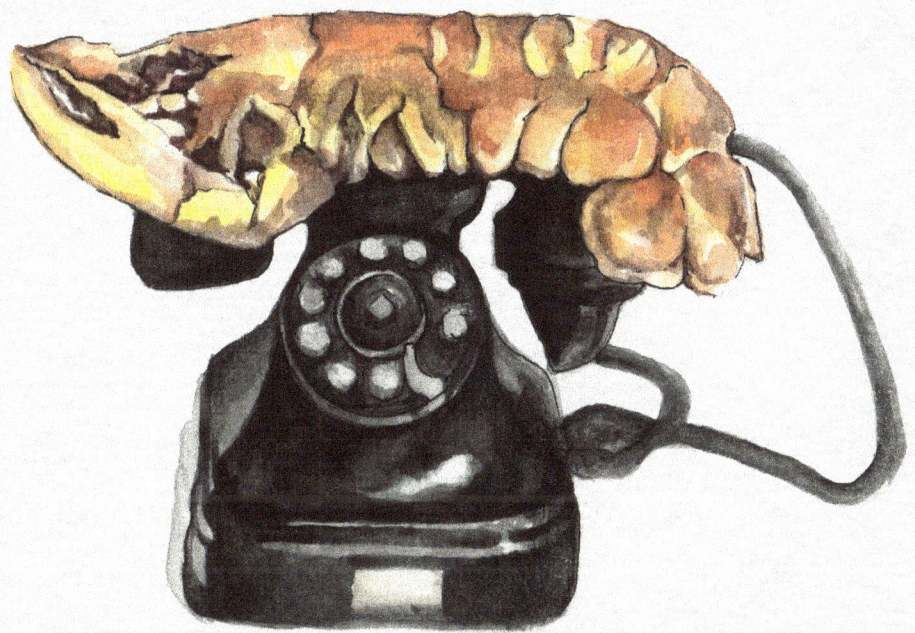

found object art

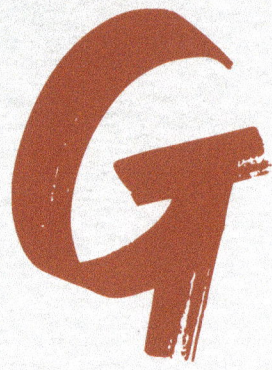

gallery

a building, room or shop where artists can display or sell their art.

genre (zhahn ruh)

a general category of an art form. The broadest division of art genres could be thought to include these: architecture, sculpture, painting, literature, music, performing arts and film. But there are many art forms outside these main categories, and many within each one. For example, within the main genre of painting there are many specialized genres, such as portrait, landscape, still life or historical painting. From French *genre*, "a kind."

geometric shape

any shape such as a circle, ellipse, triangle, square, rectangle, octagon, and so on. (Compare *organic shape*.)

gesso (JESS-oh)

a white liquid or paste used as a base coat on a canvas or panel to prepare it for painting on. Gesso protects the surface while providing a layer that allows the paint to enter and hold well to the surface.

gesture drawing

quick studies of the human form in which the artist works to capture with simple lines the essence of the pose or movement of a model, or of people involved in any action. Done in seconds or just a few minutes, gesture drawing is used to train an artist in perceiving, understanding and drawing the human form—its muscles, movements and proportions. It can also be used as a "warm-up" to a more in-depth figure drawing session.
(Compare *figure drawing*.)

glaze

in ceramics, a glaze is a substance used to paint a piece after its initial firing. The glaze is baked onto the piece in a second firing, forming a smooth, shiny, glass-like surface.

In painting, a glaze is a thin layer of paint applied over a dried layer of paint to slightly alter or enhance colors and create depth. It can be made with diluted watercolor, oil or acrylic paint. In this definition, a glaze can also be called a *wash*.

Gothic art

 a style of architecture and visual art that developed through Europe, starting in France in the 1200s. Most Gothic art was religious in nature and can still be seen in beautiful ornate cathedrals, their murals and stained-glass windows, and handmade or woodcut-printed Bibles and prayer books. Paintings, illustrations and sculptures of this period began to be more realistic, expressive, and include some depth or perspective. The term *Gothic* was created in the Renaissance as a derogatory term for art and architecture of this period because it was considered barbaric, like the Goths (northern Europeans) who had invaded Rome and destroyed its art and culture.

gouache (gwash)

a type of watercolor paint that is thicker and more opaque (less transparent) than regular watercolors.

gouge

a gouge is a chisel with a curved blade. It is used to carve or make grooves in woodwork, sculpture and ceramics. There are many sizes of gouges as well as different types of curved blades.

gradation

the gradual transition from one color, value, texture or size to another, which can help create the illusion of depth, distance or volume.

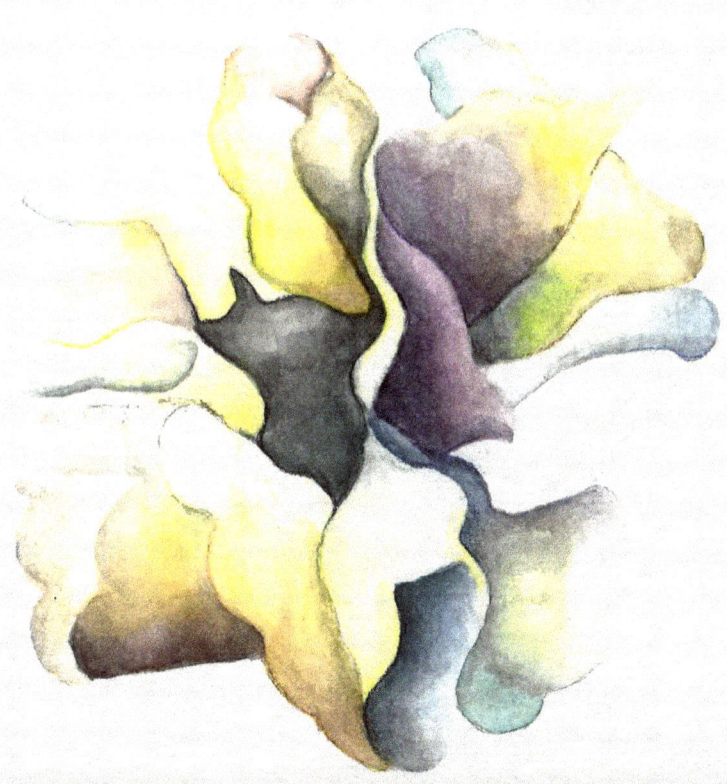

graffiti art

or *street art*

a style of art that became popular on the streets of New York in the 1970s as artists secretly painted the sides of buildings and walls of subway stations and trains. Graffiti art ranges from brightly colored, stylized letters with depth and shading, to dancing people, and even political statements. Early examples of graffiti artists were the Americans Jean-Michel Basquiat and Keith Haring. More recently, an anonymous England-based artist called Banksy and the American artist Barry McGee have become leaders in this art form.

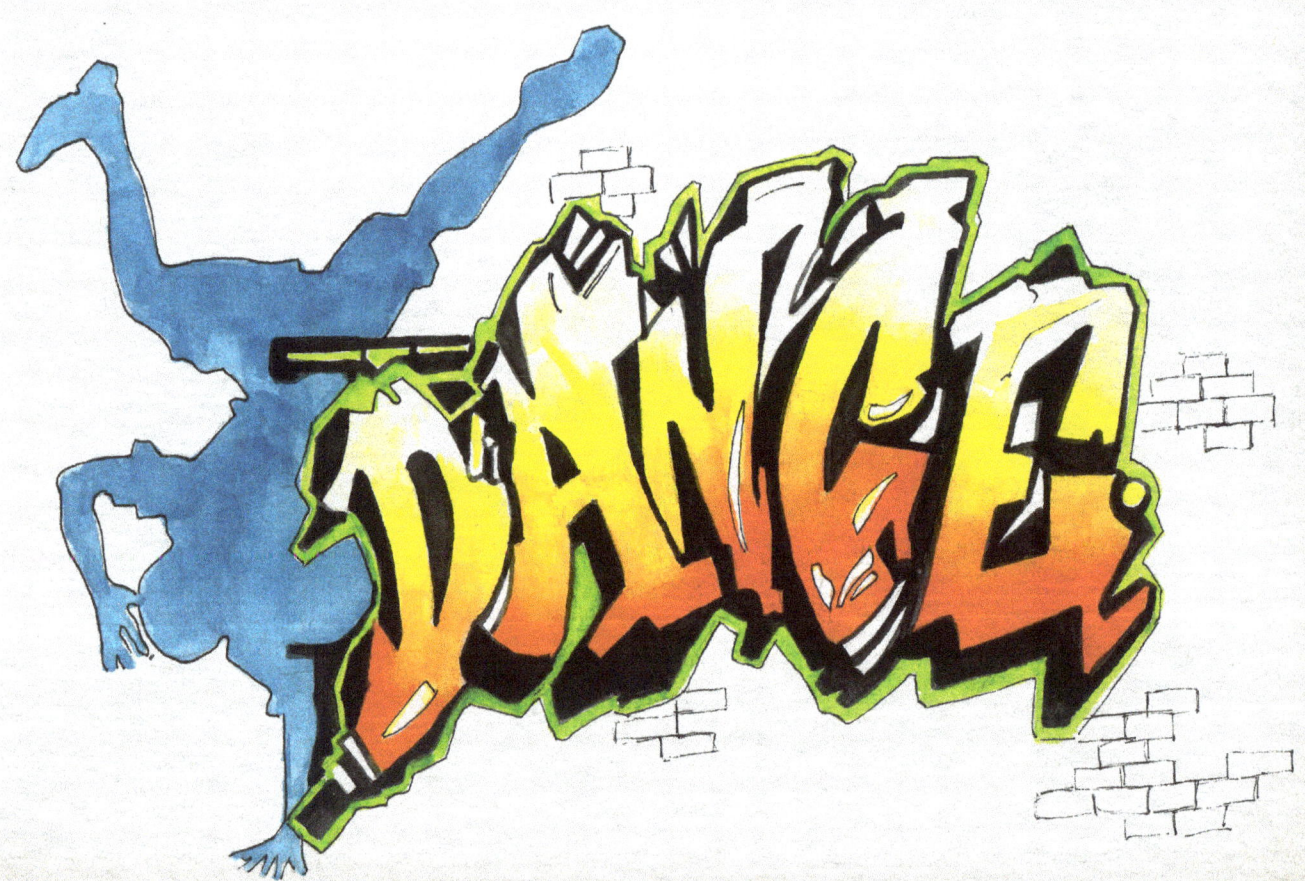

graphite

a metallic-gray crystal form of carbon, used in pencils.
Though normally called *lead,* it contains none of the heavy
metal element of that name. It comes in varying degrees of
softness and hardness and can be removed with an eraser.
(See *drawing pencils.*)

guild

through much of civilized history, people of various
professions within a city formed groups for a number of
reasons including the sharing and controlling of knowledge,
skills, trade and product quality. These groups were often
called guilds. Today, guilds of various types exist in many
fields of the visual arts. They are generally formed by artists
within a geographical area to share ideas, workspace,
materials and instruction.

H

a label on a pencil showing that the lead is hard.
(See *drawing pencils.*)

HB

a label on a pencil showing that the lead is between hard
and soft. (See *drawing pencils.*)

hatching

See *cross hatching.*

haut relief (OH ree LEEF)
or *high relief*

See *relief sculpture.*

high contrast

See *contrast.*

highlight

See *shadow and light types.*

historical painting

or *history painting*

a type of painting that is of historical, biblical or mythological figures, usually with a message of struggle, heroism or morality.

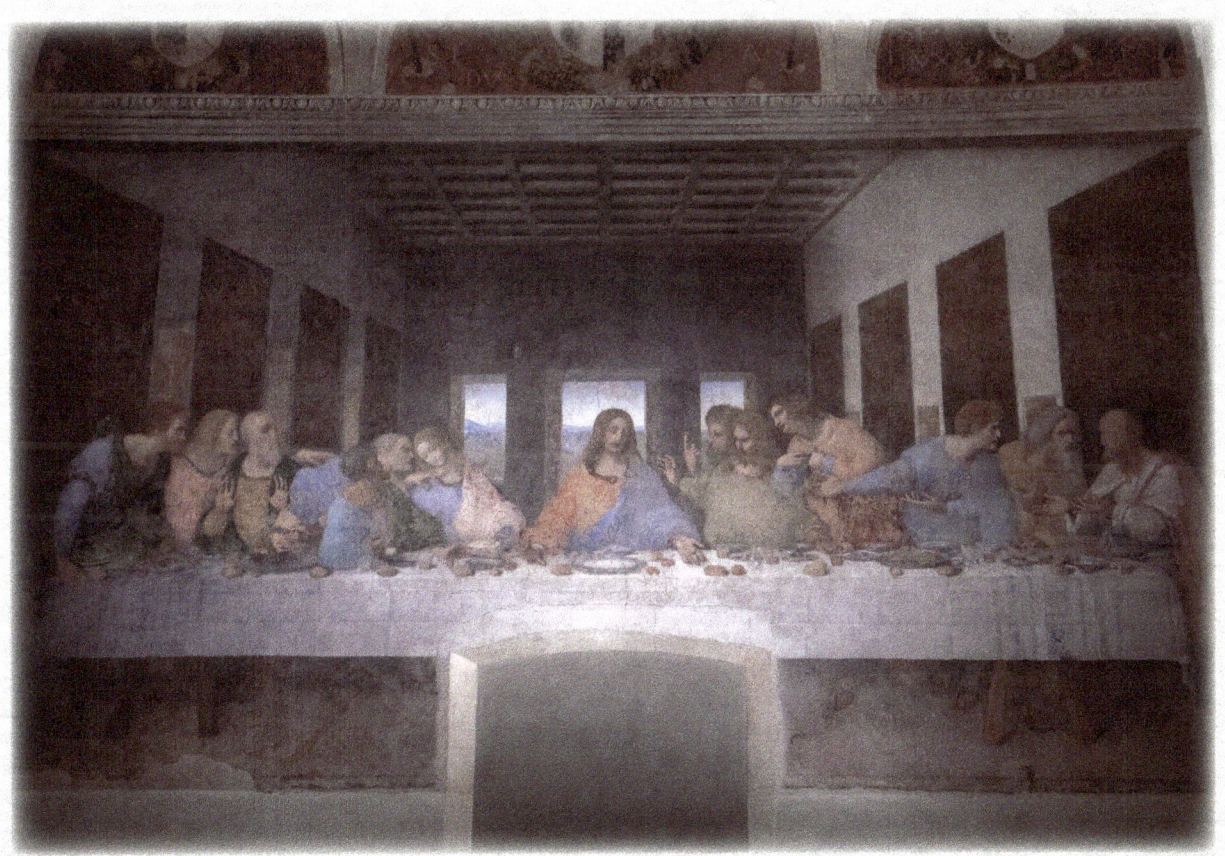

Hudson River school

over several decades in the mid-1800s, a growing number of American landscape painters broke from European traditions to create their own path in celebration of the beauty of the American landscape. Early participants came from and painted scenes of untouched wilderness in the Hudson River Valley north of New York City. Artists considered part of this movement captured landscapes in other areas of the U.S. as well. Well-known artists of this group included Thomas Doughty and Frederic Edwin Church.

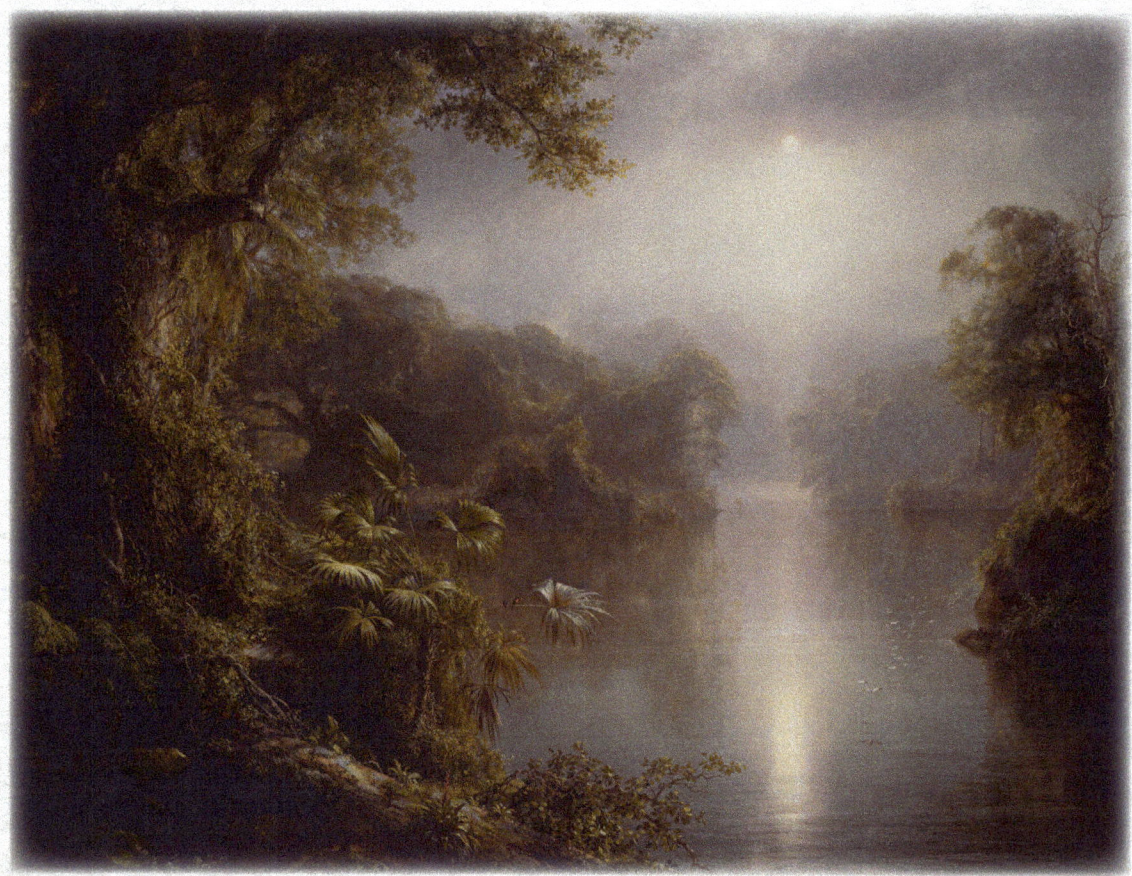

hue

the color, such as red, orange, yellow, green, blue or violet.
Note that hue refers to colors on the color wheel, so does not
include black or white. (Compare *tone.*)

hyper-realism
or *photo-realism*

an art movement which appeared in the 1970s that sought
to imitate and almost surpass reality by showing even the
smallest details of a subject, such as skin pores. Paintings in
this style can be so detailed that they look like photographs.
This style is also used in sculpture where the pieces create
the illusion of an actual person, animal or object.
From *hyper,* "beyond, above, extreme" + *realism.*

illustration

drawings or paintings that are meant to go together with a certain text to explain or enhance it, such as illustrations for a book on human anatomy, a textbook on types of trees, or a book of children's stories.

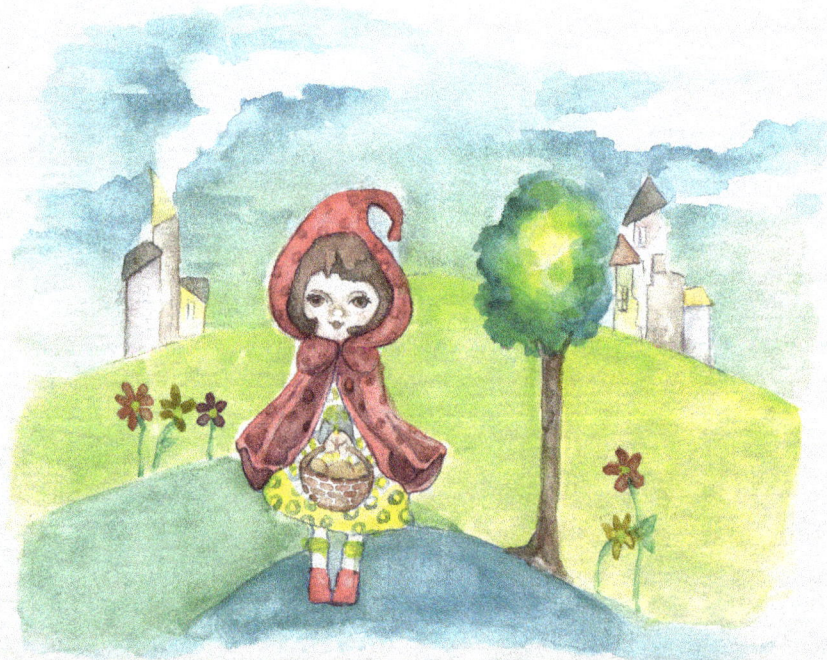

impasto

the technique of applying paint thickly, whether with a brush or palette knife. When dry, the paint stands out from the canvas and gives the painting definite texture, as the brush or knife strokes are clearly visible. From Italian *im-,* "upon" and *pasta,* "paste."

impressionism

an art movement that developed in France in the late 1800s. After years of working from sketches inside dark studios, a group of artists decided to go outside and paint landscapes and scenes from direct observation. This forced them to work quickly as they tried to capture the momentary changes of light, shadow and hue. The result was art that lacked precise details but was rich with motion, light and radiant colors. Because the paintings looked more like visual impressions than realistic interpretations of the landscape or subject, the term impressionism came into use. The first impressionistic painters of this influential movement were the French artists Claude Monet, Auguste Renoir, Edgar Degas and Paul Cézanne.

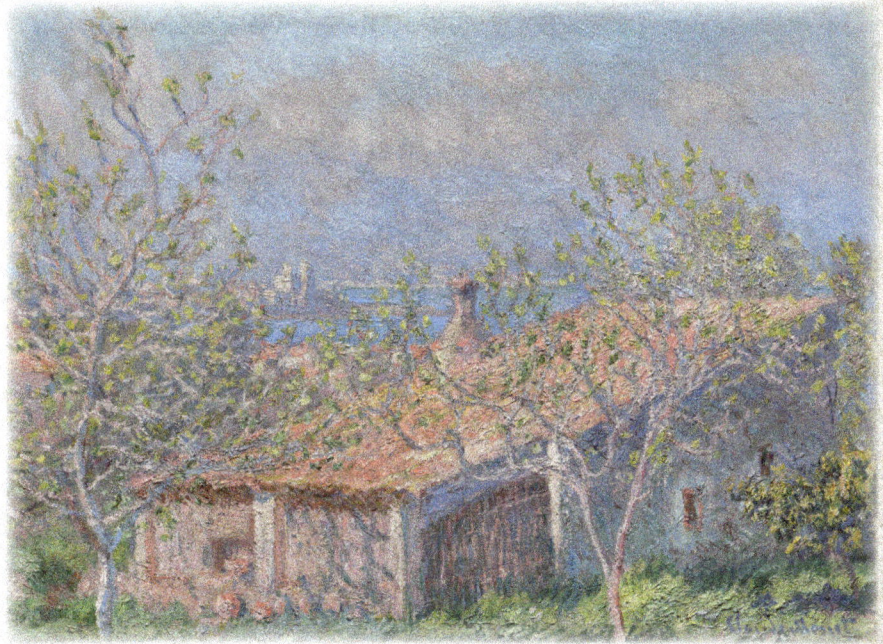

inclination

the inclination of a line means how it leans or what its angle is. All diagonal lines have some inclination.

industrial design

designing products that will be mass-produced and used by many people, such as cars, toys, appliances and electronics. Industrial design considers efficiency and functionality in addition to aesthetic qualities.

ink

a writing or drawing medium, usually black or brown, in liquid or paste form. The most common type of ink is made of carbon diluted in a liquid.

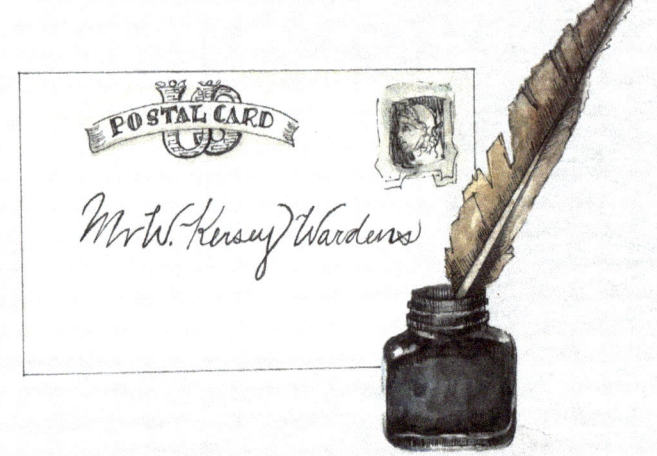

installation art

large works of art constructed with a variety of materials and designed for a specific location. Installation art can be temporary or permanent. It is meant to transform a space in some way and offer a more interactive experience for the viewer.

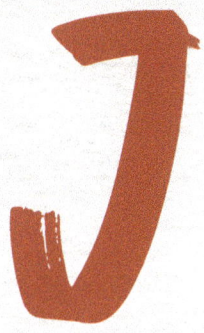

junk art

a category of found object art, in which the artist makes sculptures or artwork using trash or junk. (See *found object art*.)

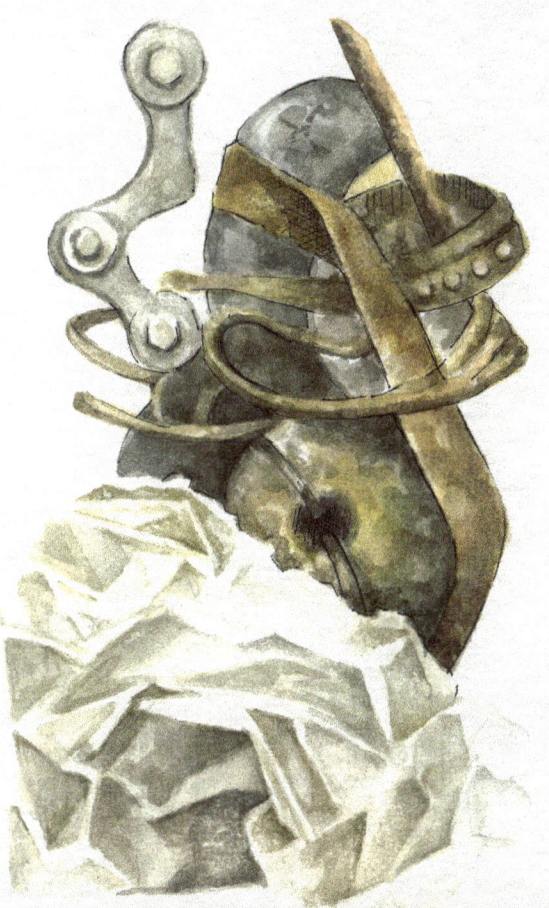

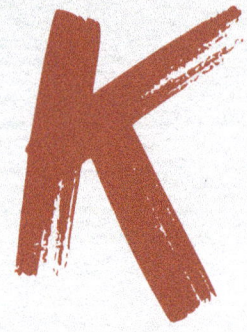

kiln

a special type of oven designed to get hot enough to bake pottery, bricks or clay objects, or to enable a chemical reaction to take place as occurs with the hardening of a glaze.

kinetic art

art which is designed to move as part of its artistic effect, such as a mobile that is moved by air or a sculpture with motion caused by a motor.

land art

See *environmental art.*

landscape painting

paintings in which scenery and nature are the subject matter.

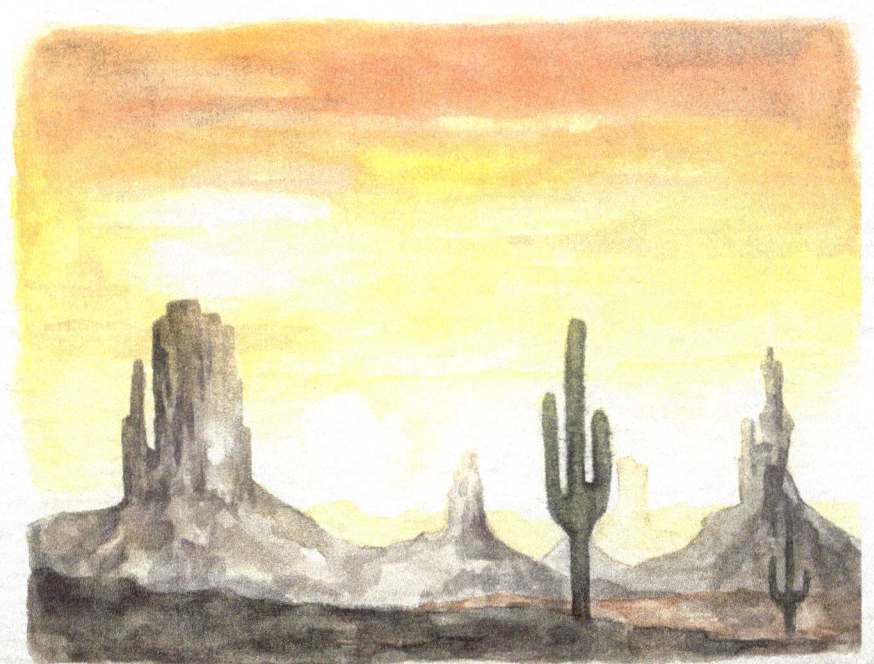

lead

See *graphite.*

leather-hard

in ceramics, a specific stage of the drying process of a clay object when it is still a bit moist, but it has dried enough to be handled or carved.

life drawing

drawing from a live human model. (See *figure drawing.*)

light art

an art form which utilizes light as its main medium, whether the light is neon, fluorescent, LED, laser or natural.

limited edition

See *edition.*

line

a line is defined as a mark made in any direction. A line is essentially a moving point. It is considered the beginning of any drawing.

line drawing

a drawing made using lines, generally with no attention to shading or color.

line quality

refers to the thickness of the lines used in a drawing. Lines of varying thickness are used to help suggest lighting, weight and even distance, increasing realism.

linear perspective

a method for creating the illusion of distance by using lines and points as guides to draw things which look smaller in the distance and gradually larger as they "approach" the viewer. (See *one-point perspective*, *two-point perspective* and *three-point perspective*.)

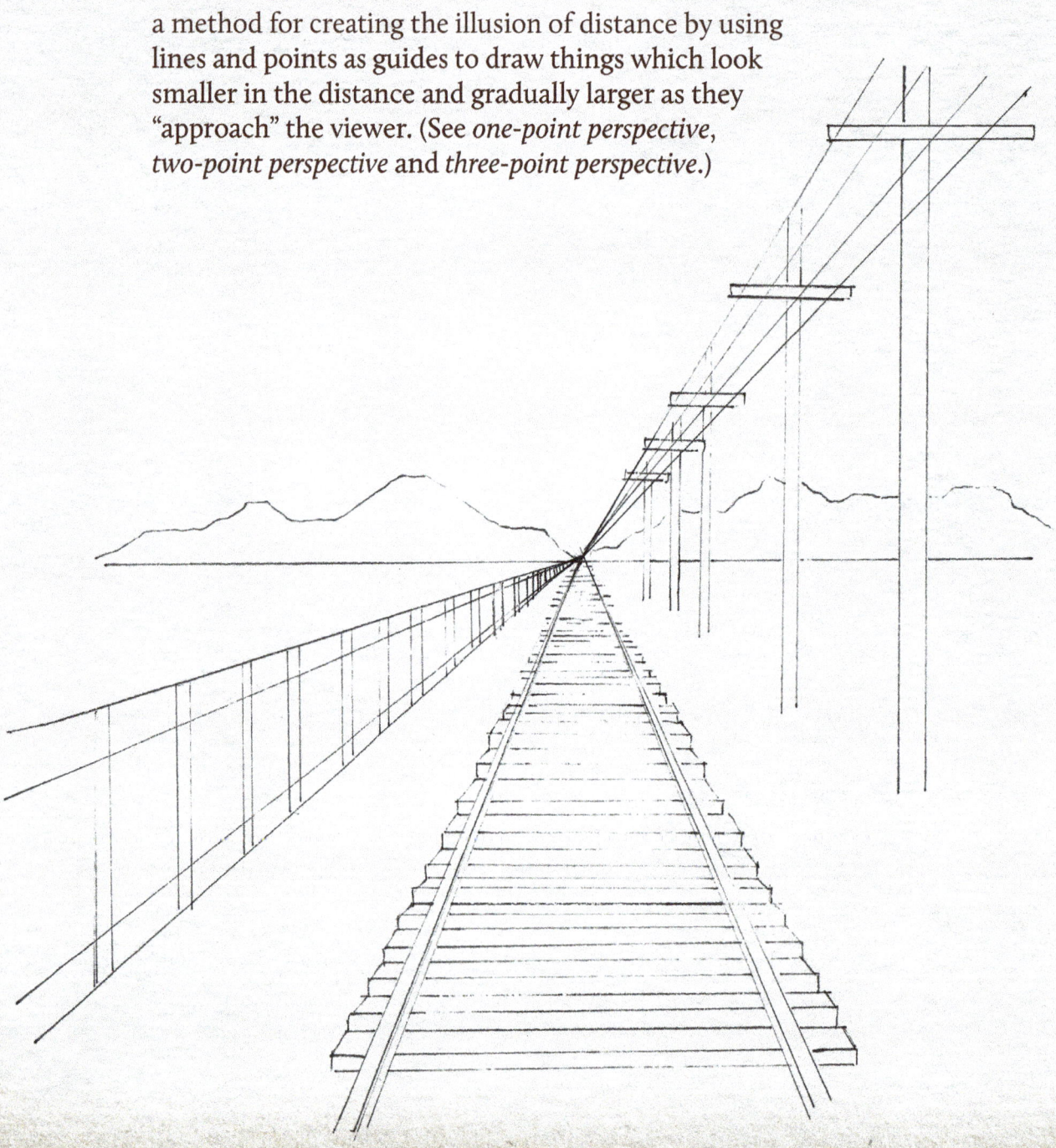

linocut

a print made from an engraved piece of linoleum (a durable, easy-to-clean, flat substance commonly used to cover floors) that has been mounted to a block of wood. The term can also refer to the etched design itself.

linseed oil

a pale yellow oil, commonly used in making oil paints. Additionally, different types of linseed oil can be added as a medium to dilute oil paints, increase gloss (shine) and speed or slow drying time. It can also be combined with other mediums, such as turpentine or spike lavender oil. Linseed oil is made from the seeds of the flax plant, a plant with small blue flowers, the slender stems of which are used to make cloth.

lithograph

a method of printmaking based on the fact that water and oil do not mix. The artist draws on a stone or metal plate with a greasy (oil-based) crayon. When ink is applied to the plate and then washed off, it sticks to the drawing only. On printing, the inked image then transfers to the paper.

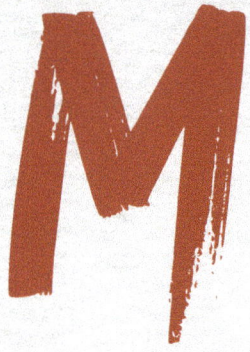

marble

a very hard type of stone for carving and sculpting. Many of the greatest sculptors in history have chosen marble for their sculptures because when it is first taken out of the quarry, it is relatively soft and easy to carve, but as it ages, it hardens and has great endurance. Additionally, when polished, it achieves a beautiful translucent quality.

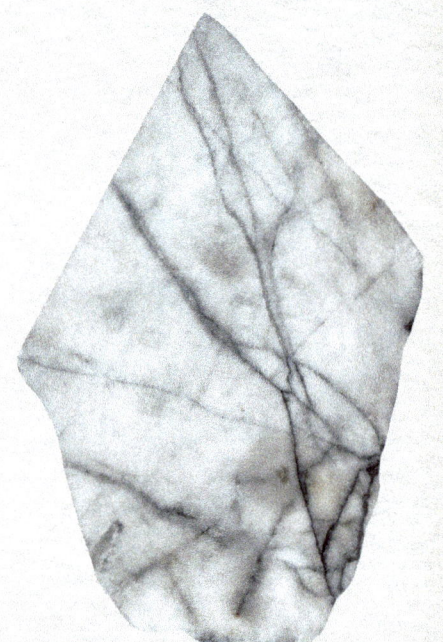

master

an expert in a certain field. In art, a master is an artist who has achieved great mastery or skill.

masterpiece

artwork which is considered outstandingly good or skilled. Also, a person's greatest achievement or work.

mat

a piece of cardboard or cardboard-like material acting as a border around a drawing, painting or print. It normally goes between the artwork and frame but can also function as a frame itself.

matte

describes a surface that reflects little light and lacks highlights. A matte surface absorbs more light than a shiny surface. Matte surfaces also show less contrast between darks and lights.

media

plural of *medium.*

medium

the materials or method an artist uses such as oil, pastel, watercolor, printmaking, ceramics, etc.

In painting, a medium is the liquid used to mix with pigment to make paint or to thin paint already mixed. For example, in oil painting, a common medium is linseed oil, whereas in watercolor the medium is simply water.

mid tone

See *shadow and light types.*

miniature

a very small painting or drawing in any medium, usually ranging from 1.5 to 10 inches in size.

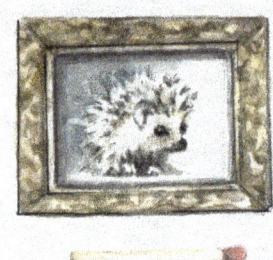

minimalism

a style of art where the piece is reduced to its simplest possible form. It seeks to eliminate or simplify things like color, texture and subject matter. A metal cube would be an example of a minimalist work of art. This style emerged in New York in the late 1950s and 60s. Some of the most famous minimalists of the time were the American artists Frank Stella, Ellsworth Kelly and Donald Judd, and Russian artist Kazimir Malevich.

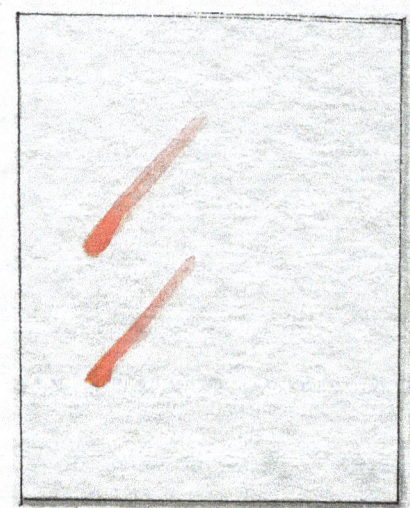

mixed media

the use of different materials within the same work of art;
for example, a piece created with digital art and watercolor,
or a piece combining collage and oil paint.

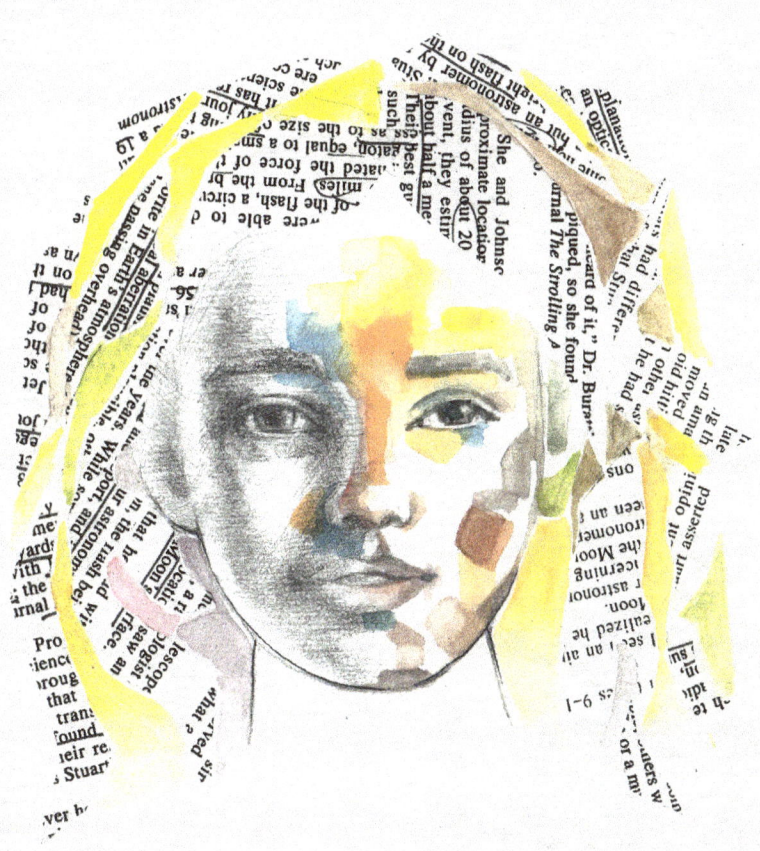

mobile

a sculpture that typically hangs from wires or strings so that it is moved by air currents. These types of sculptures were first originated in 1932 by the American artist Alexander Calder.

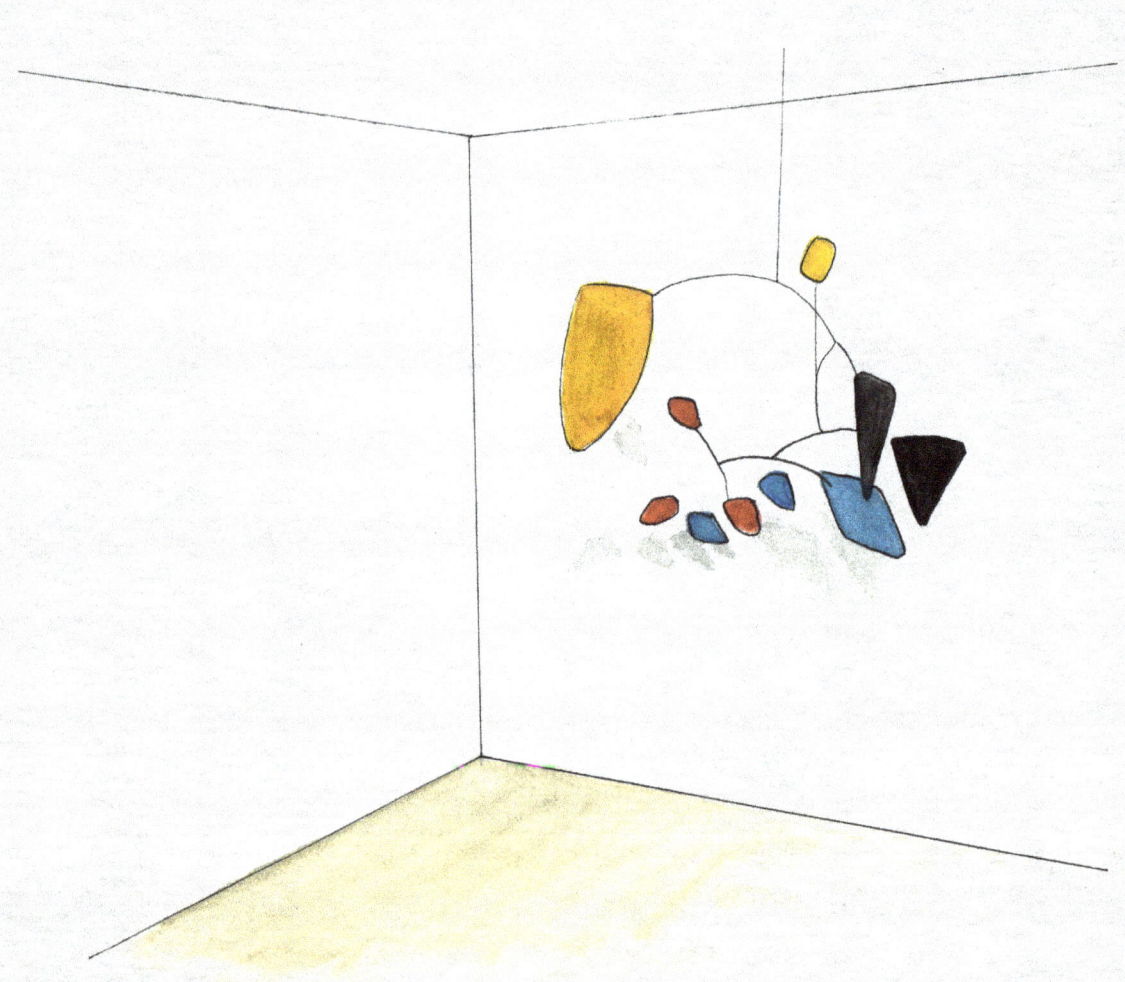

modeling

building up pieces of clay, wax or another soft material to create a desired form.

modern art

a term still used to describe the period of art that started with impressionism in the late 1800s and continued roughly through World War II. The period after this is generally referred to as *contemporary art.*

monochrome

artwork that uses varying tones of only one color, or shades of black and white. From Greek *mono-*, "one" + *khromatos*, "color."

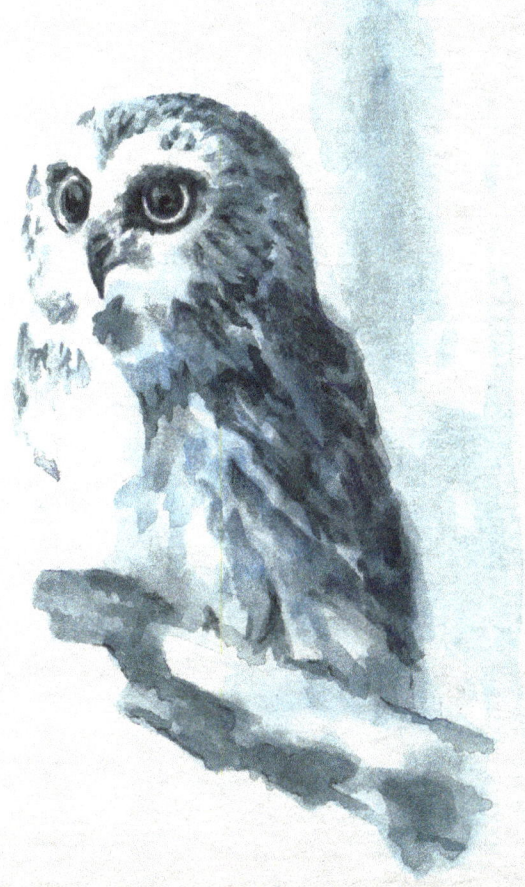

montage

a piece of art put together from different images (usually photographic) tied together by some overall theme or message. The term can also refer to a rapid sequence of film shots put together.

mosaic art

art made up of many small pieces of glass, ceramics, stone or other items glued to a surface.

mural painting

the creation of paintings, often large, directly on a wall or ceiling.

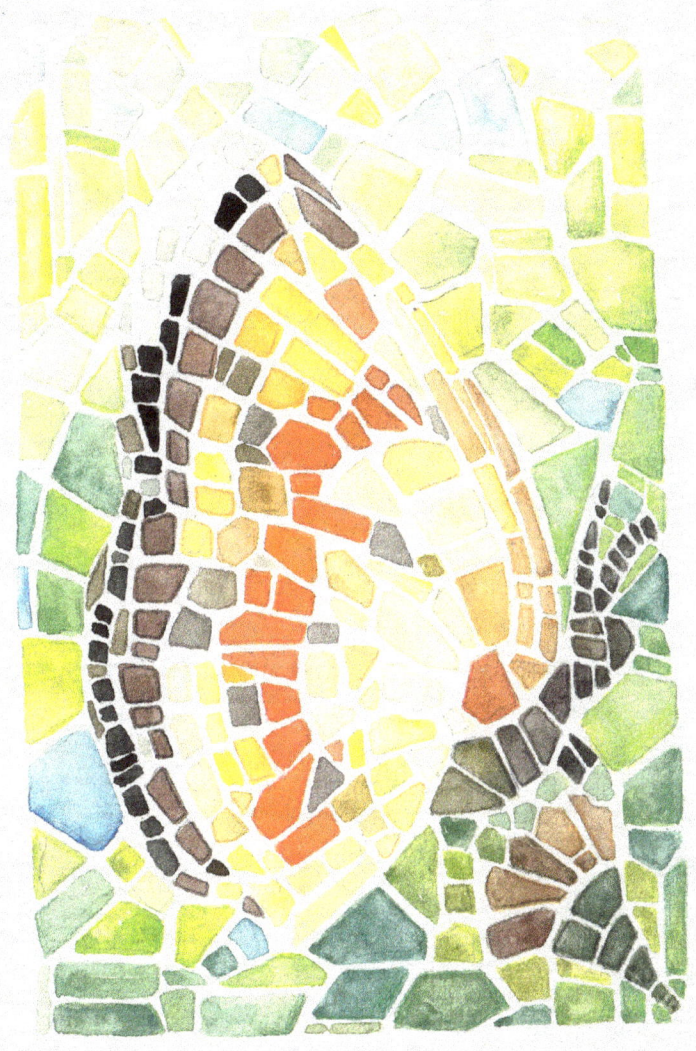

mosaic art

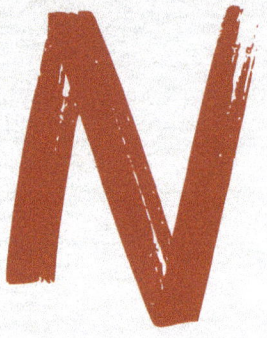

naive painting (ny EEV)

a style of painting that looks like it has been done by a child. It is frequently associated with artists who have not had formal art training. Some of the most important naive artists of the 1900s included the French artists Henri Rousseau and André Bauchant, and Alfred Wallis who came from Cornwall in southwest England. From French *naïve*, "simple, natural," from *nāsci*, "to be born."

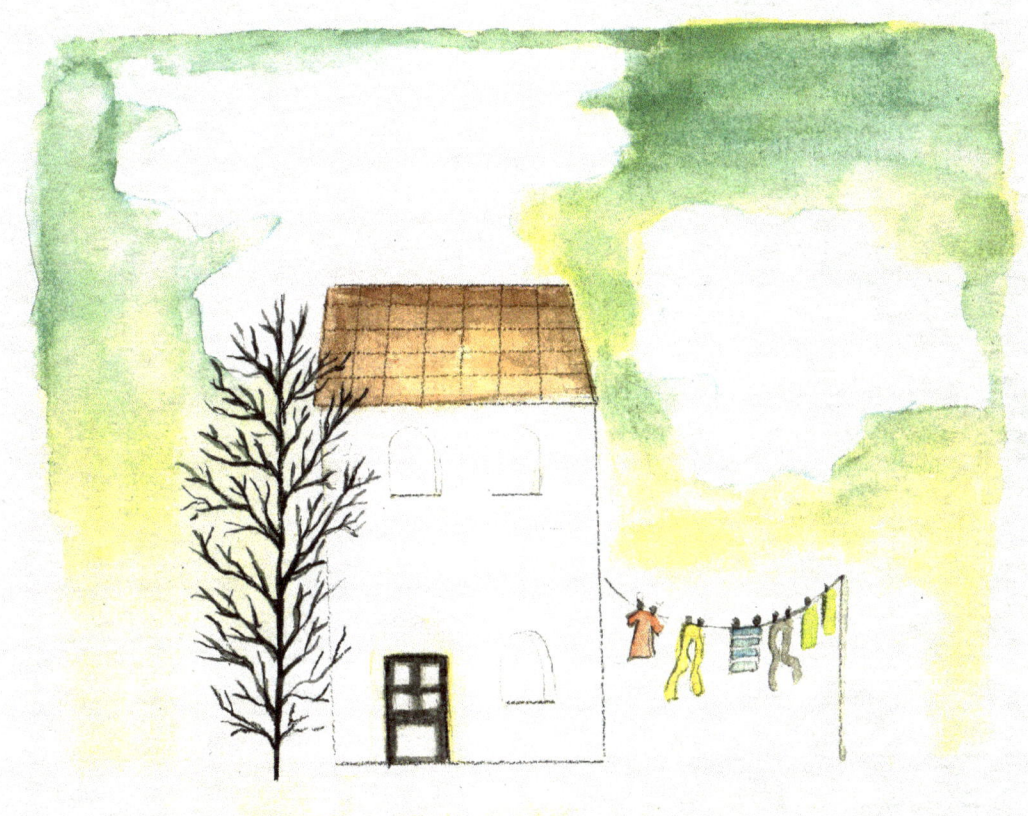

nature art

See *environmental art*.

negative space

the space of a piece of art that is not the main subject or object; the area or areas that surround and help define the solid matter of the primary shape or shapes. (Compare *positive space*.)

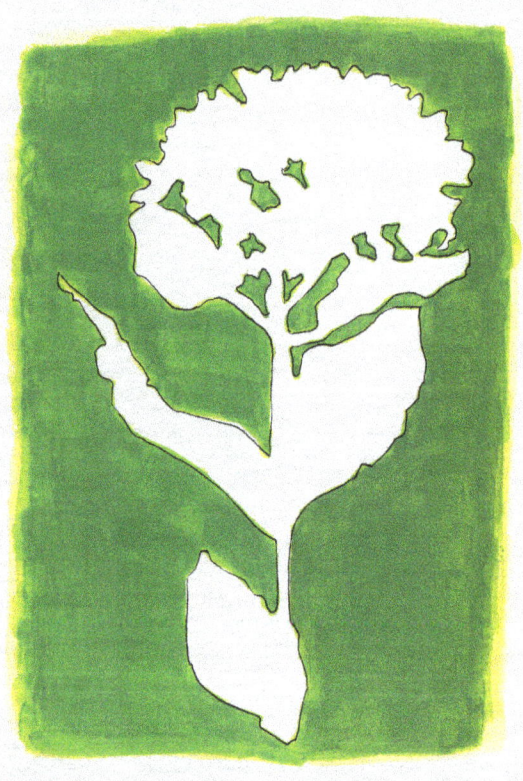 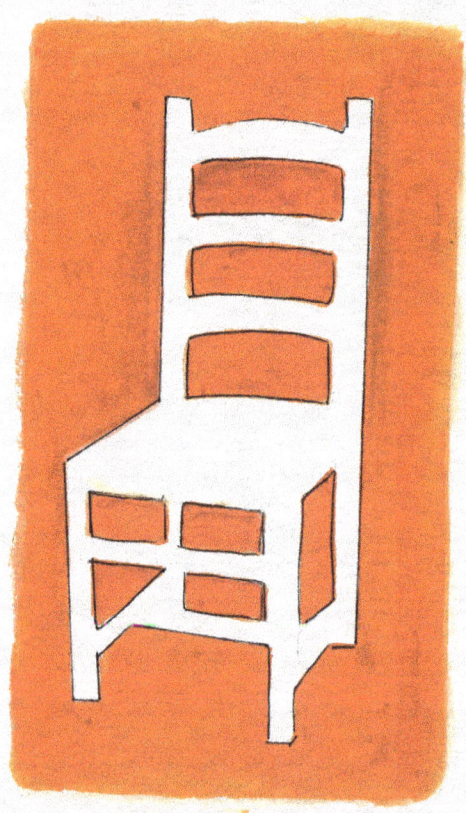

neutral colors

a broader term for *earth tones,* neutral tones or colors are more subdued (softer, milder, less strong) or more muted (quieter, less loud or bright) than colors such as red, yellow, blue, etc. They tend toward brown, gray, off-white or black. They can be created by adding a complementary color, white, black or gray, or some combination of these, to a pure or bright color.

neutralize

dull a color's brilliance and make it darker by adding its complementary color. For example, to make red darker, less vibrant, less "red," you can add its complement—green.

Notan

a Japanese design concept that uses a balance, or harmony, of flat, light and dark areas. Also an art form using paper cutting and positive and negative space. (See *positive space* and *negative space*.)

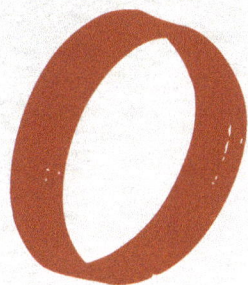

occlusion shadow

See *shadow and light types.*

oil paint

a type of paint which is made of color pigments mixed with an oil base. Because of its oily nature, it is a slow-drying paint which allows artists to blend, make corrections and develop the painting gradually over a period of days.

old master

a term used to refer to great artists of earlier times, most often those of the Renaissance or baroque period such as Michelangelo or Rembrandt.

one-point perspective

a drawing technique that uses one vanishing point on the horizon, used for things like roads, railroad tracks, tunnels or hallways when viewed straight-on, not from the side or an angle. (Compare *two-point perspective* and *three-point perspective*.)

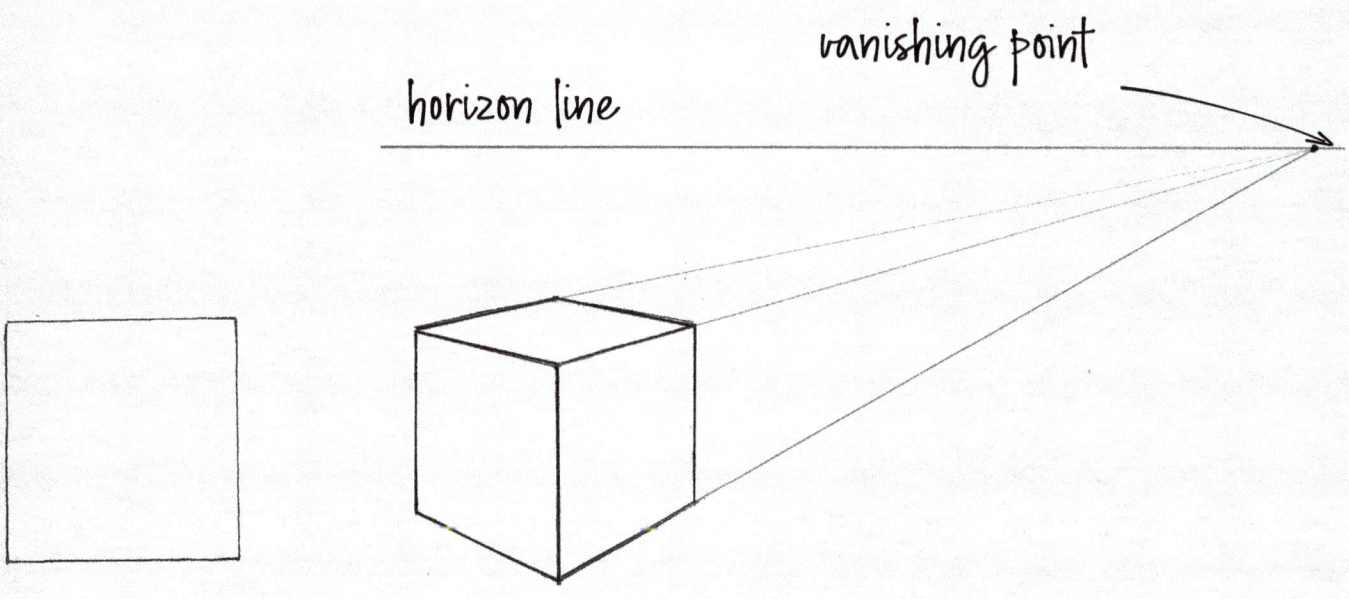

opacity

the degree to which you cannot see through something.
(Compare *transparency.*)

opaque

the quality of a substance that does not let light pass
through it; not transparent.

organic shape

shapes more closely resembling those found in nature.
The word organic in this sense means, "relating to or
coming from living things." They have no specific names,
can be partly curved or straight, and can be clearly defined
like a leaf or loosely defined like a cloud.
(Compare *geometric shape.*)

origami

the Japanese art of folding paper to create small decorative representations of objects, people, animals, etc.

outline

the outermost line of a drawing which defines its shape.

outsider art

a style of naive art which is done by people who are not considered to be part of the structured art world, such as children, prisoners or patients in institutions. Because most outsider art is not produced for professional sale, it is considered by some to be more honest and freer in spirit or intention than professional art. (Compare *naive painting*.)

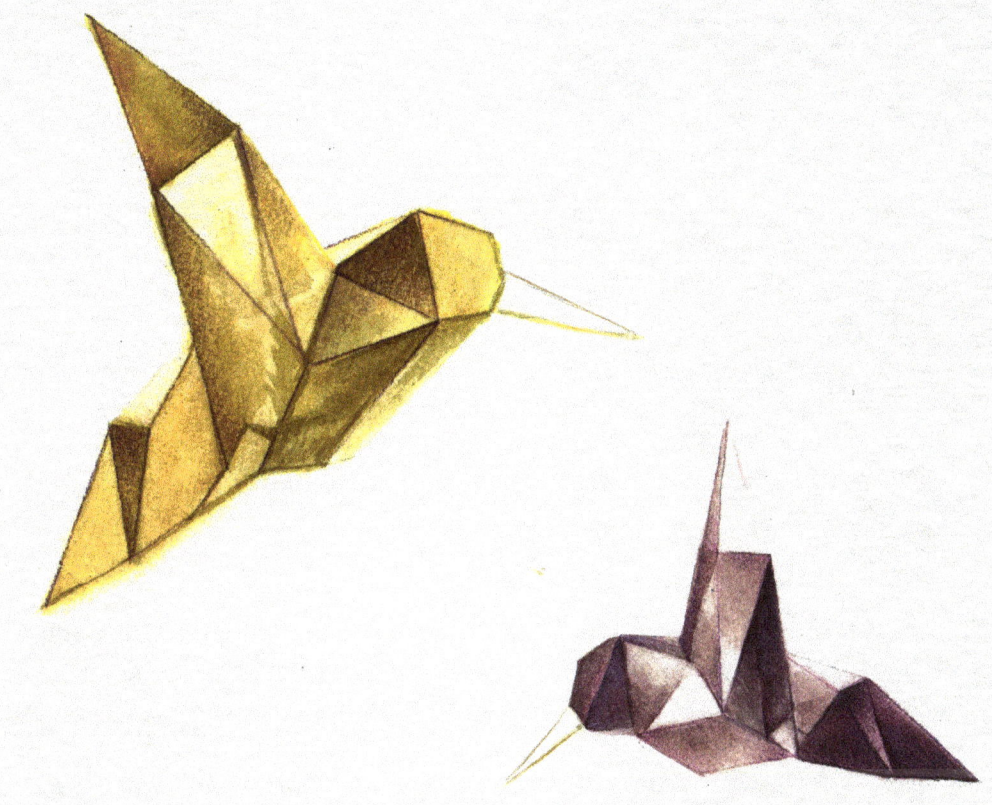

origami

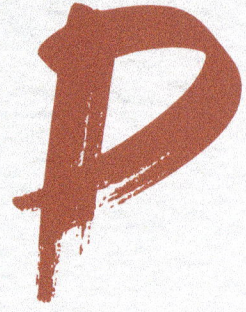

painting

the application of color to a surface through any paint medium, such as watercolor, acrylic or oil paint.

palette

a flat piece of wood, metal, plastic or glass used by the artist to arrange and mix colors while painting. Some palettes are made to be held in the hand near the surface being painted.

The word can also refer to the color range characteristic of a particular artist or style. For example, a "warm palette" refers to a piece that uses reds, oranges, yellows and browns. A "Velázquez palette" describes the use of a set of colors made popular by the Spanish painter of that name in the early 1600s.

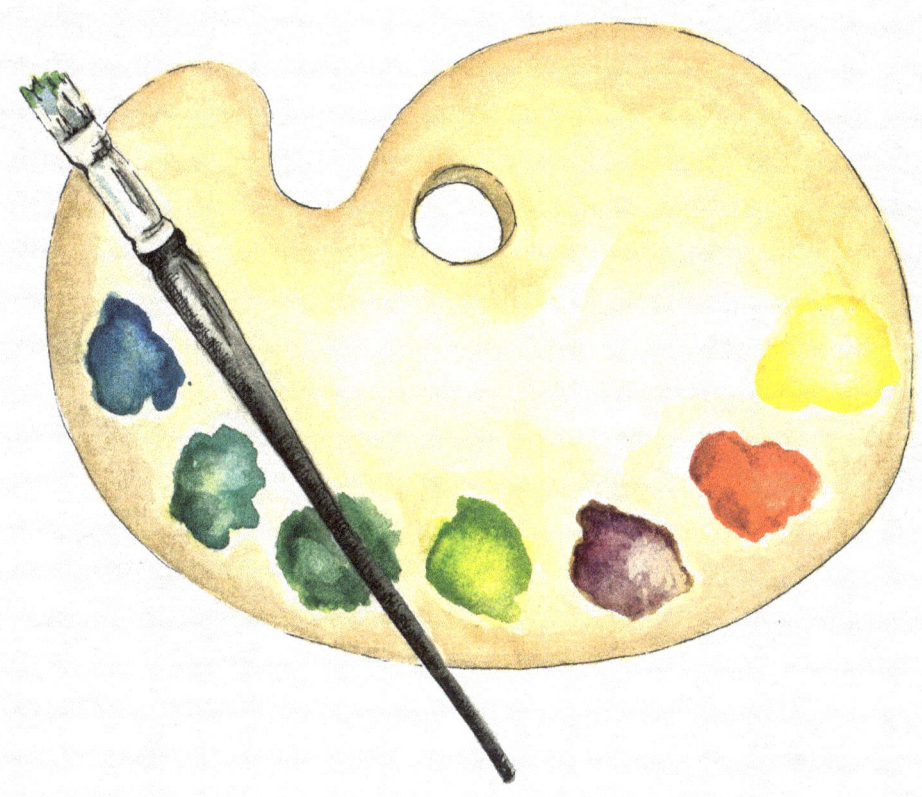

palette knife

a handheld tool with a broad, blunt blade for mixing colors on a palette or for applying them directly to a painting in thick layers. Some are shaped more specifically for applying paint to a canvas and are called *painting knives.* Many artists refer to all of these, of whatever shape, as palette knives.

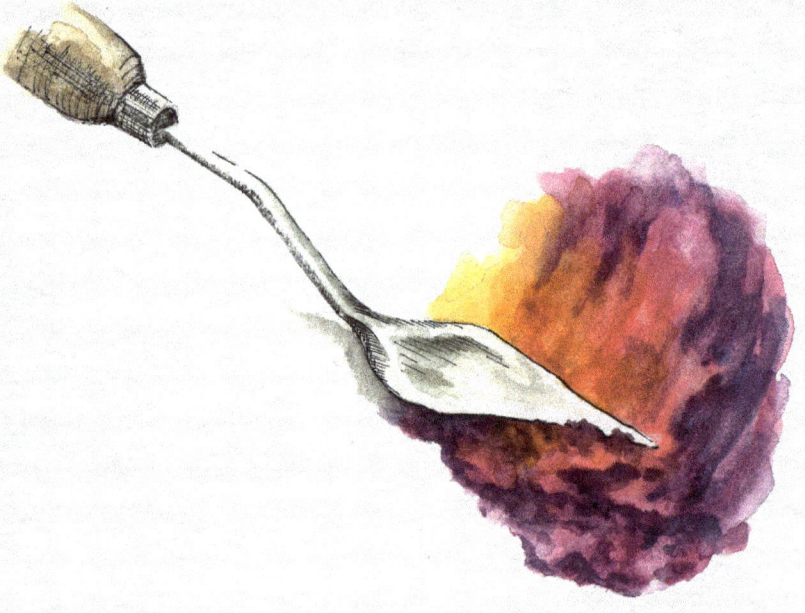

panel

a rigid surface, usually of wood, on which to make a painting, used instead of a canvas.

paper

a material usually made from breaking down wood into a wet mass of fiber, pressing it into thin sheets, and drying it. It can then be used for drawing, writing, wrapping, cutting and many other things. There are many different kinds of paper designed for specific art media.

papier-maché (pah pee ay mah shay)
or *paper-maché*

a material for molding sculptures made of paper scraps or strips and some sort of glue. It is molded while wet, often with the support of wire or other light material that will give the sculpture its shape. It then dries hard and can be painted on. An inexpensive art form, the glue can be made from water and flour and the paper strips cut from most any paper that would otherwise be thrown away or recycled.

pastel

a type of artist's crayon. There are three main types: hard pastels, soft pastels and oil pastels. Hard pastels and soft pastels are both made from pressing together color pigment, chalk and a type of glue or binder. Hard pastels are powdery and bright, behaving much like chalk. They can be used for finer lines. Soft pastels are less powdery, richer in color and easier to blend. Oil pastels are made of color pigment and plant-based oils. They are similar to soft pastels but have an even softer, waxier consistency.

patina (PAT uh nuh, or puh TEE nuh)

a thin layer of green or brown coloring on some or all of the surface of bronze sculptures. This effect can be produced with chemicals applied by the artist or it can occur naturally due to chemical changes caused by the weather.

patron

a person who supports the arts and may even provide financial support to one or more artists throughout their careers.

pattern

an arrangement of repeating colors, lines or shapes.

performance art

art which is created by actions the artist performs and may include other media or elements. It is a type of conceptual art. Though sometimes similar, it means something different than *performing arts,* which refers to the more traditional art forms of acting, singing, and dancing.

perspective

the word perspective comes from Latin *per,* "through" and *specere,* "to look." In art, perspective is about creating the illusion of looking at a three-dimensional scene even though it's actually just a flat surface, such as a drawing or painting. Different techniques for creating perspective are used to create the illusion that you are closer to certain elements within the piece and further away from others. (See *aerial perspective*, *linear perspective*, *one-point perspective*, *two-point perspective* and *three-point perspective*.)

photography

images made using a camera. Light enters a camera through the lens and is focused onto a light sensitive material (film camera) or a sensor (digital camera). From these, prints can be made.

pigment

a colored powder, usually extracted from plants or minerals but also chemically produced, which is mixed with water, oil, egg or glue to create paints, pastels, colored pencils and so on.

pixel

the smallest unit of illumination on a digital display that can be given a separate color. Pixels are combined to create images, text or anything visible on a screen. The more pixels, the larger the image can be while remaining sharp.

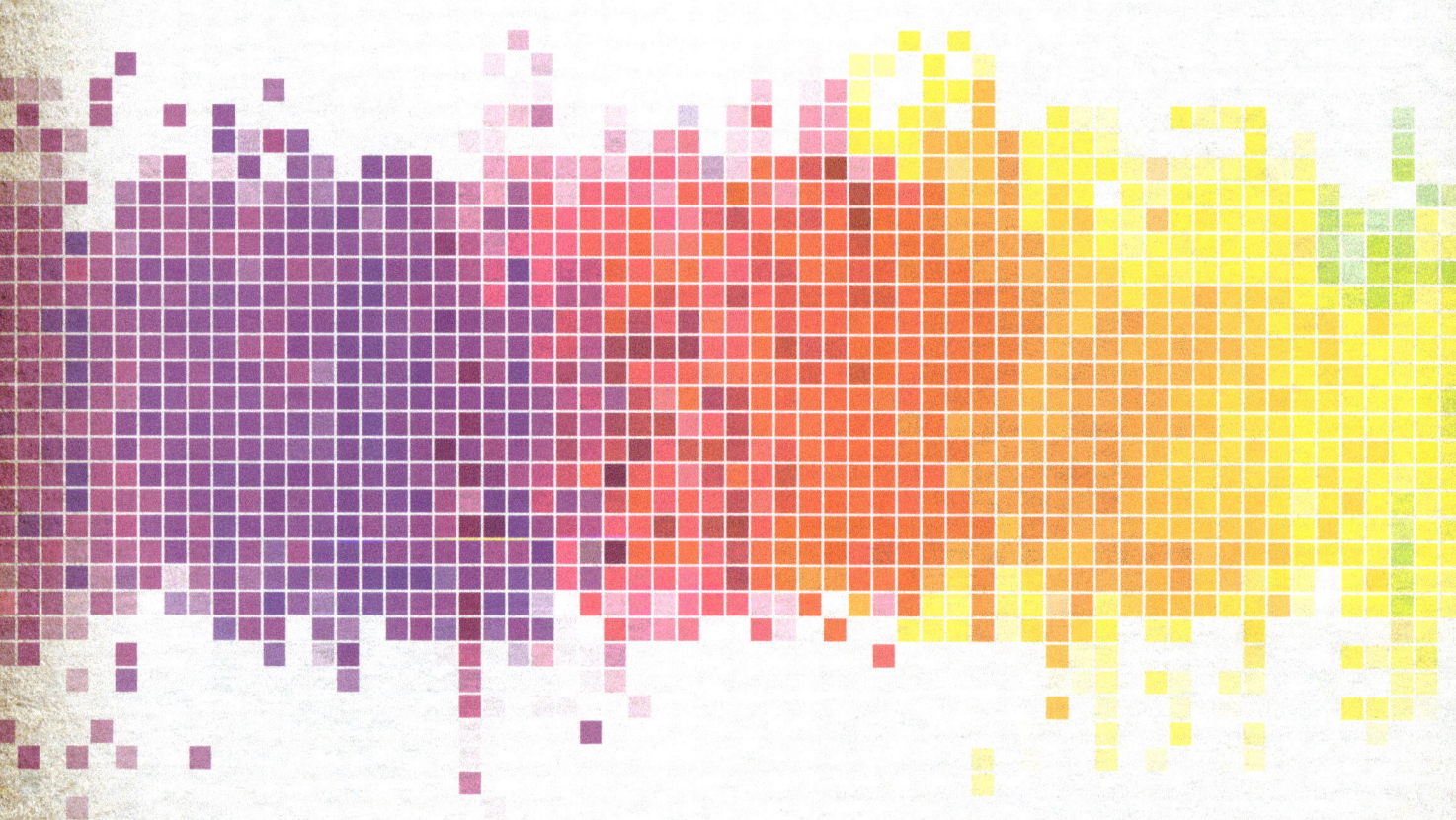

plane

a plane is a flat side of anything. In painting, drawing or particularly sculpture, a plane can refer to any area of a surface that is facing a particular direction, even if it is not flat.

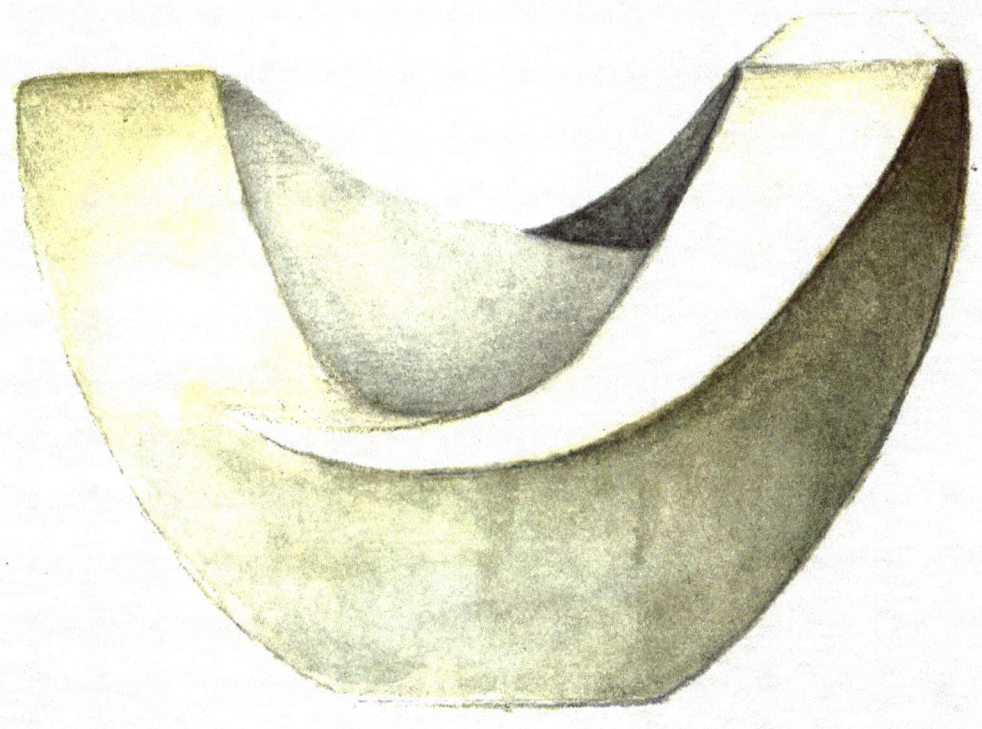

plein-air painting

painting done outdoors, usually of a natural landscape, made popular by artists of the French impressionist movement. From French *en plein air*, "in the open air."

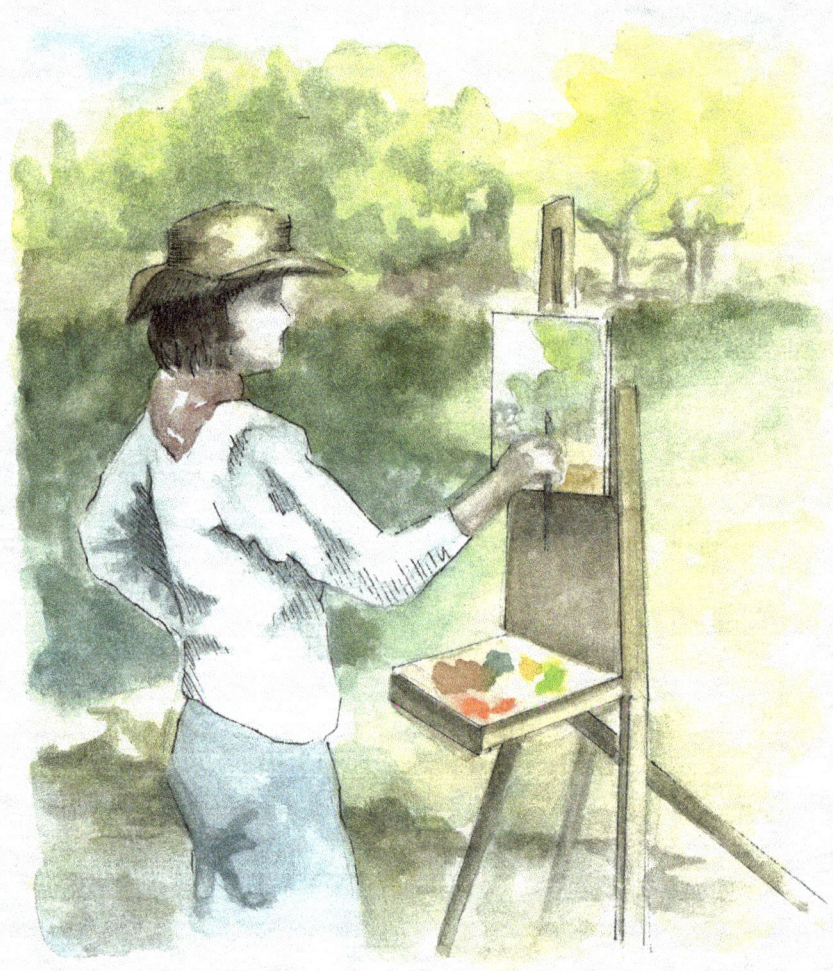

pointillism

a technique developed in the late 1800s as an extension of *impressionism* in which a painting was created by the artist using small dots of color on the canvas. When viewed from a distance, the dots of color blend together forming the overall image of the painting. Well-known artists of this technique included the French painters Georges Seurat and Paul Signac.

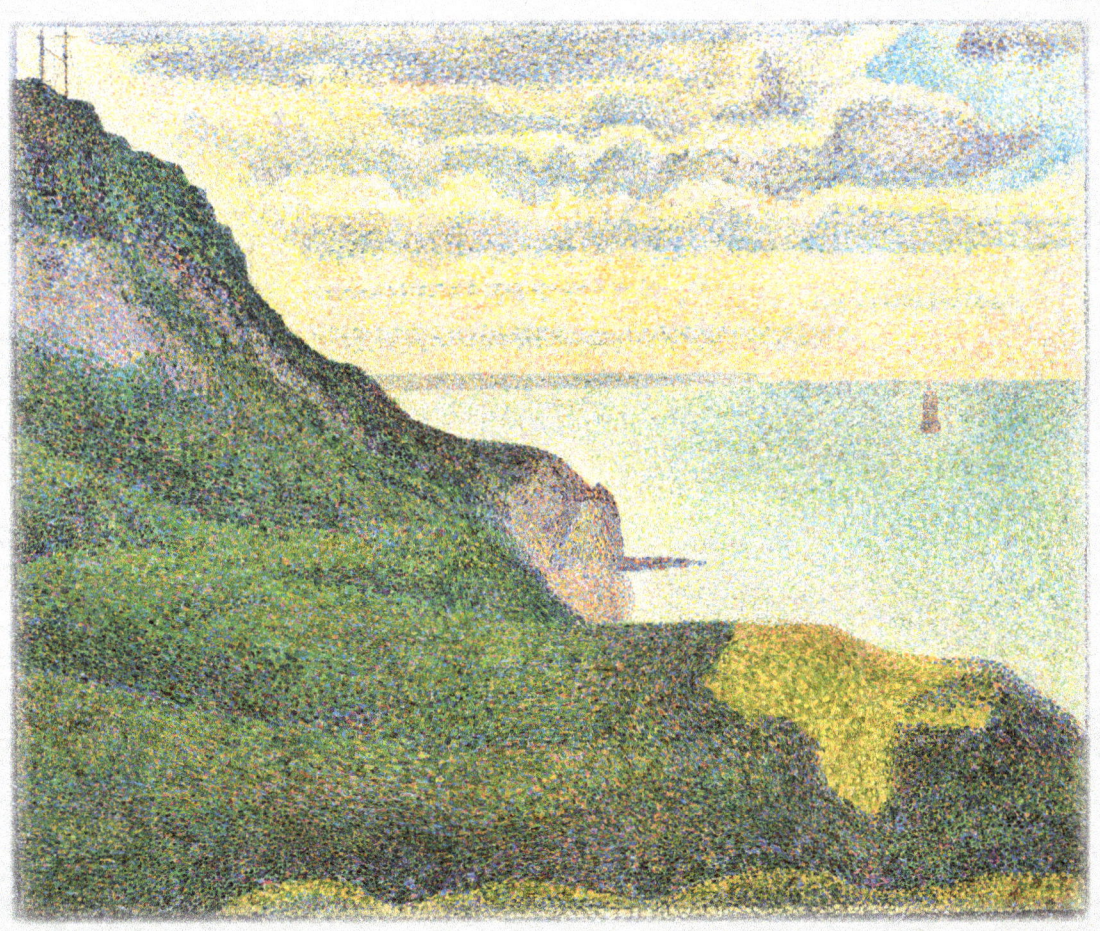

polyptych (PAHL ip tick)

a work of art consisting of more than three separate pieces which are meant to go together. (See *diptych.*)

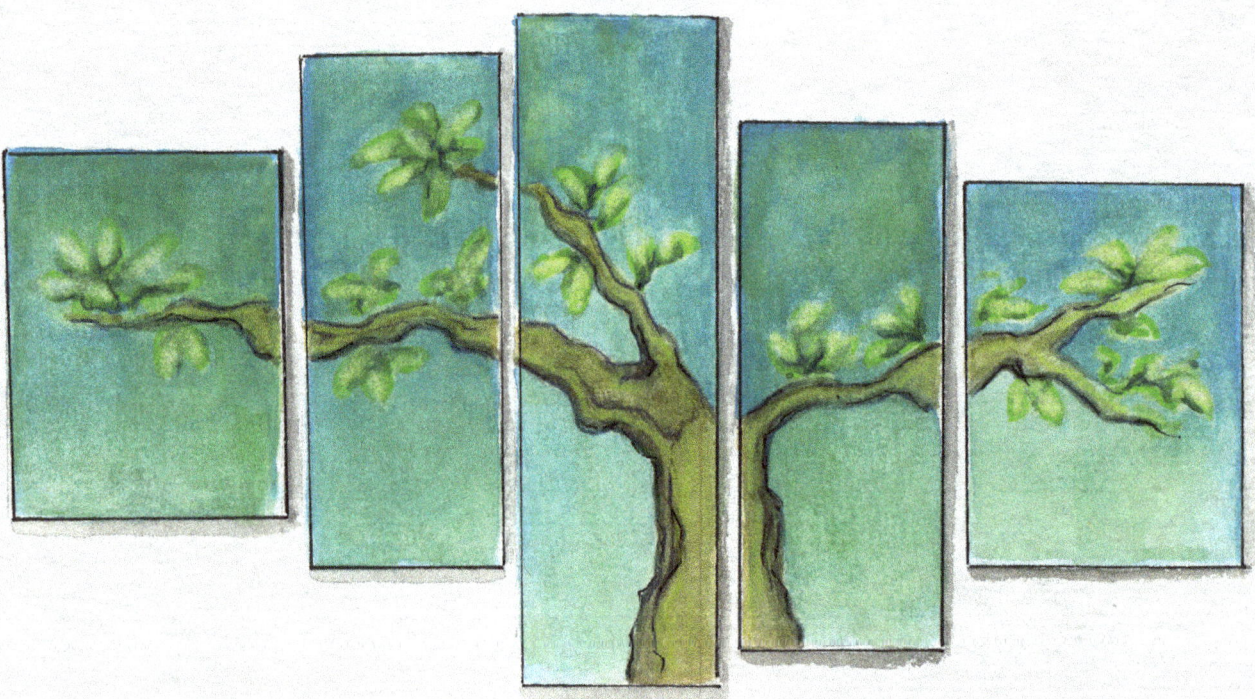

pop art

an art movement which flourished in the US and Britain in the 1960s. It began as a revolt against traditional art by young artists who felt that art in museums and galleries had nothing to do with their own lives and thus could not be related to. For inspiration, they turned to advertising, product packaging, comic books and Hollywood films. One of the most important figures of this movement was the American artist Andy Warhol, and one of his most famous works was a display of thirty-two paintings, each of a can of Campbell's soup.

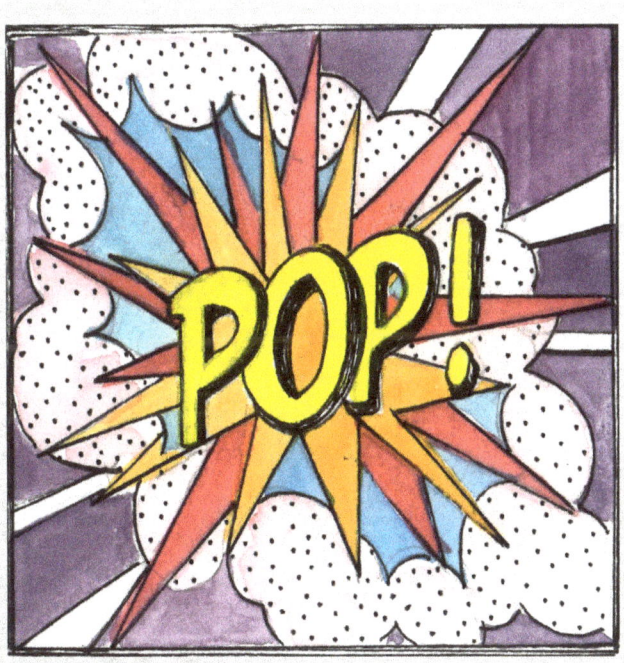
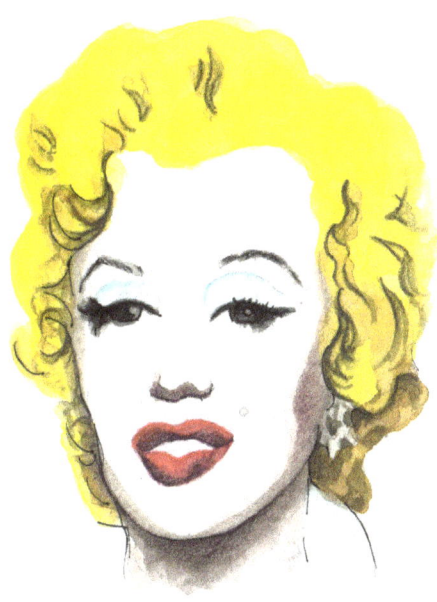

porcelain

a type of ceramics, porcelain is a fine-grained white material fired at high temperatures resulting in a delicate and somewhat translucent (see-through) product with glass-like qualities. Originating in China nearly 2000 years ago, porcelain products are often called *china* or *fine china* in the western world.

portfolio

a collection of an artist's work, or of work by several artists, for the purpose of promotion. Also, a large, flat case for carrying flat sheets of paper, such as drawings. From Italian *portare*, "carry" + *foglio*, "leaf."

portrait

a painting, drawing, sculpture, photograph or other artistic representation of a particular person or small group of people. The focus is normally on the expression, mood or personality of the person or group.

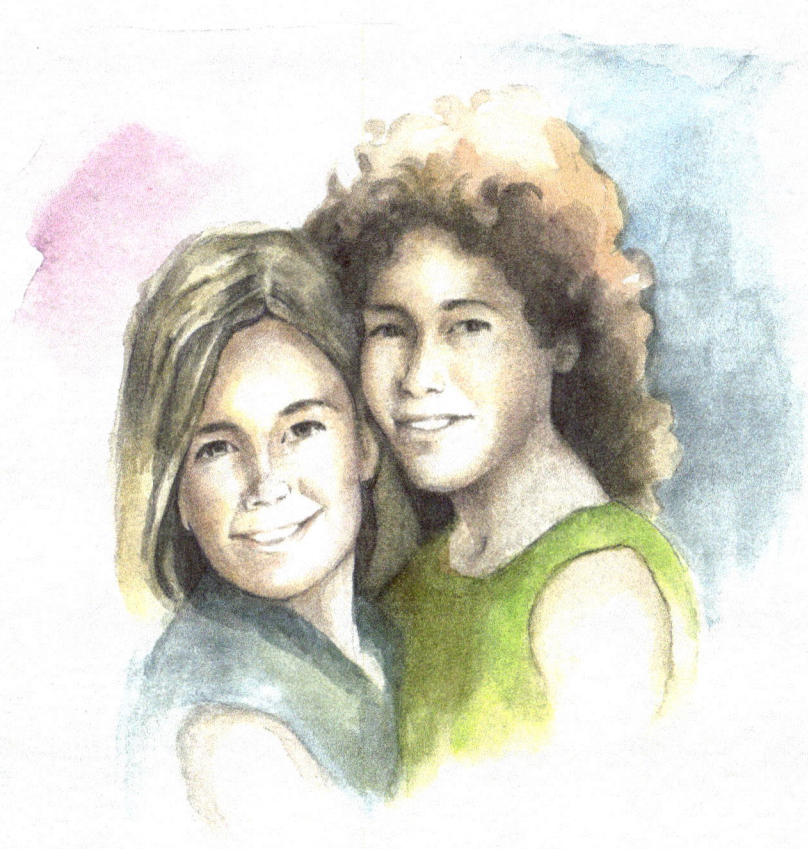

positive space

the space used up by objects in a piece; the solid matter of the primary shape or shapes in a drawing or painting. (Compare *negative space.*)

pottery

a form of ceramic art in which clay is shaped either by hand or on a pottery wheel. Often, pottery is defined as ceramic pieces made for practical purposes, such as cups, bowls, plates and vases.

pottery wheel

a machine used in ceramics for making pots. A lump of clay is placed on a round platform and, as the platform spins, the potter molds the lump into a smooth, round shape.

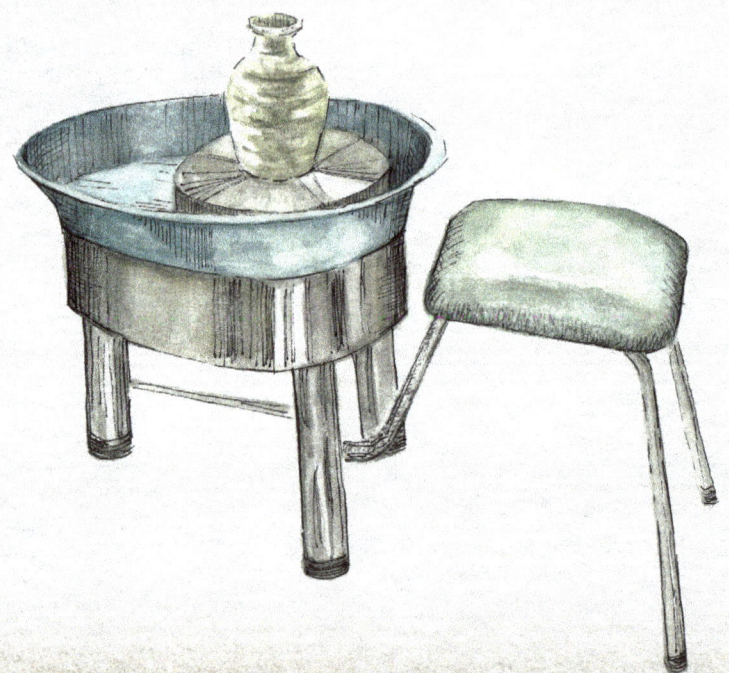

power point

See *rule of thirds.*

primary colors

red, blue and yellow. These are called primary colors because all other colors can be made from these. Primary colors cannot be made by mixing other colors.

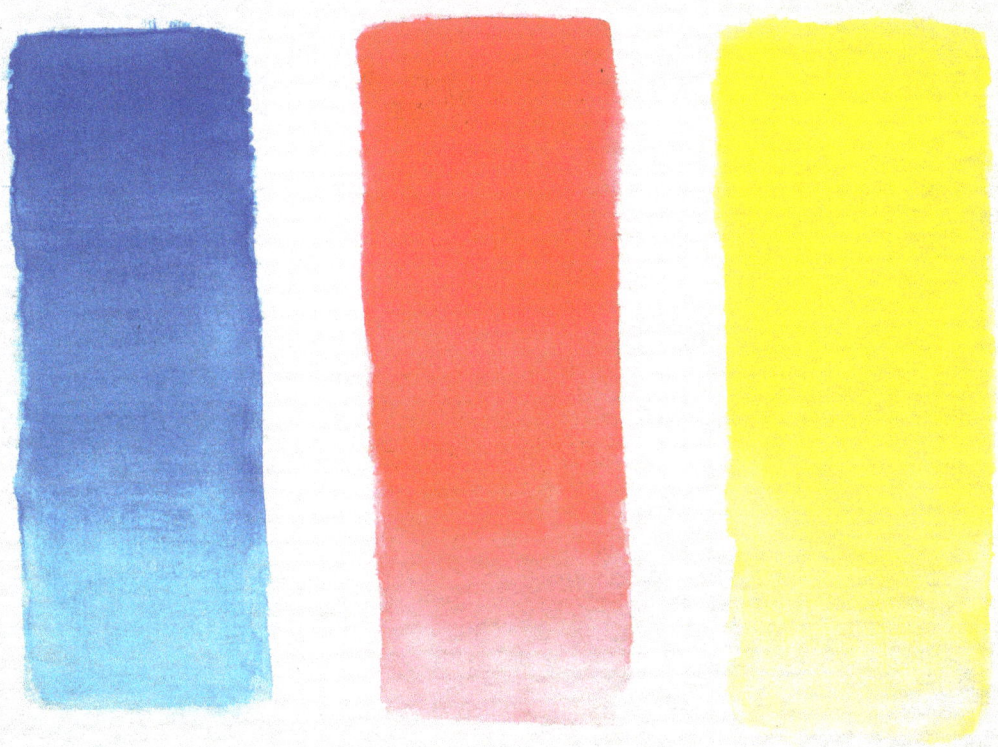

print

an image made from an etched or engraved block, stone or plate, or similar type of reproduction. There are many printing methods and techniques, including lithograph, woodcut and etching. Prints are useful in helping an artist reach a wider public because several prints can be made from one original work.

printmaking

the design and making of prints by an artist.

proof

a test print (as in photography or printmaking) created for review to determine if any adjustments need to be made.

proportion

the size relationship of one part of a whole to its other parts. For example, the parts of the human body have fairly regular proportions to one another. If a drawing or sculpture had feet or hands too large for the rest of the body, you would say they are "out of proportion."

protest art

See *activist art*.

public art

art meant for public spaces, most commonly sculpture.

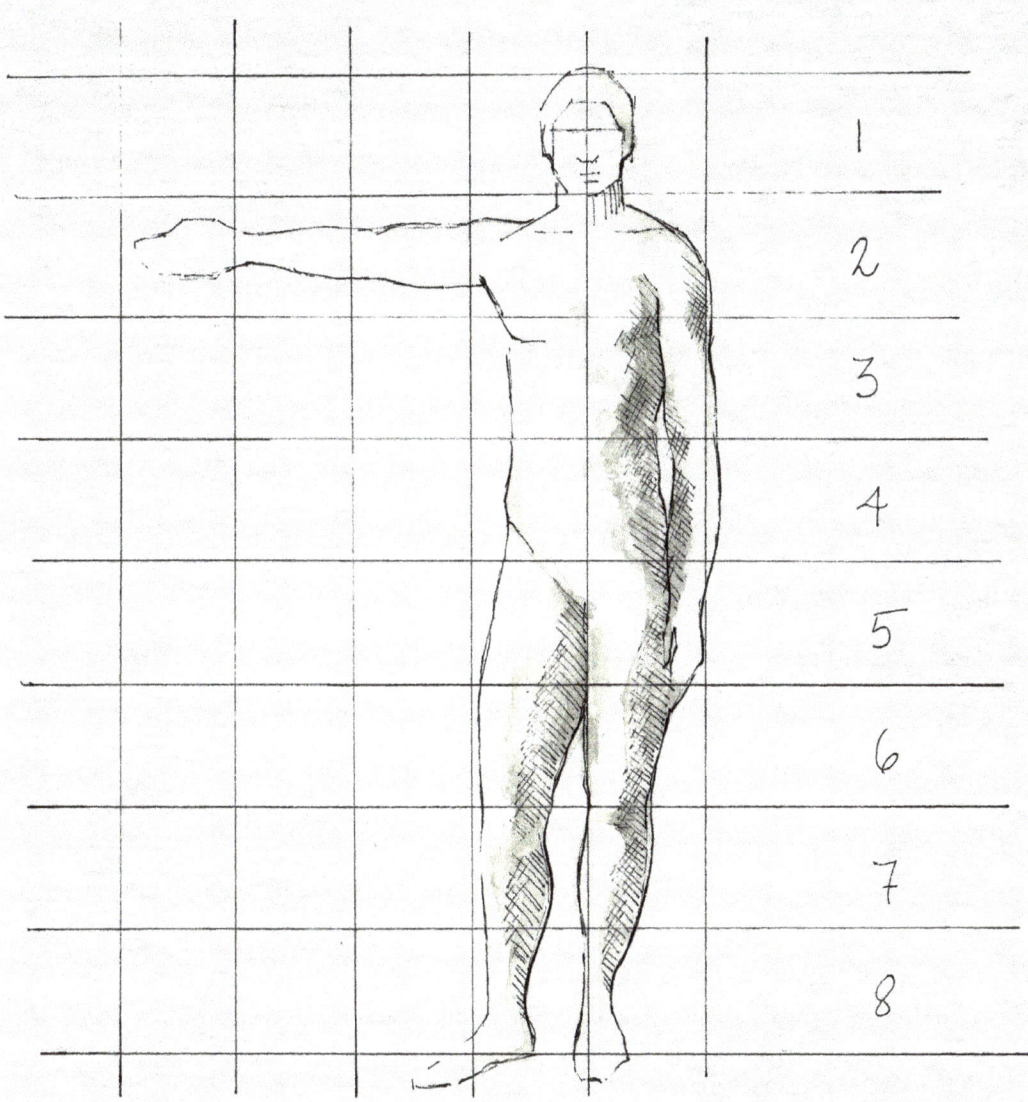

1

2

3

4

5

6

7

8

proportion

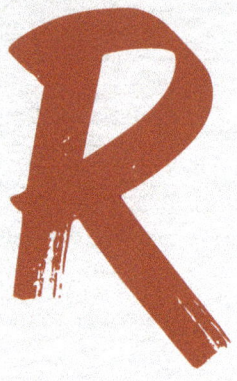

real texture

texture that is actual, where the roughness or smoothness could actually be felt with the sense of touch. Real texture exists in sculpture, textile art, thick applications of paint showing brush strokes, collage and many forms of mixed media. (Compare *simulated texture.*)

realism

a style of painting which attempts to copy, approximate or base itself in a recognizable reality. It attempts to show things as they really are. This style became a recognized movement in France in the 1850s, led by French painters Gustave Courbet and Jean-François Millet.

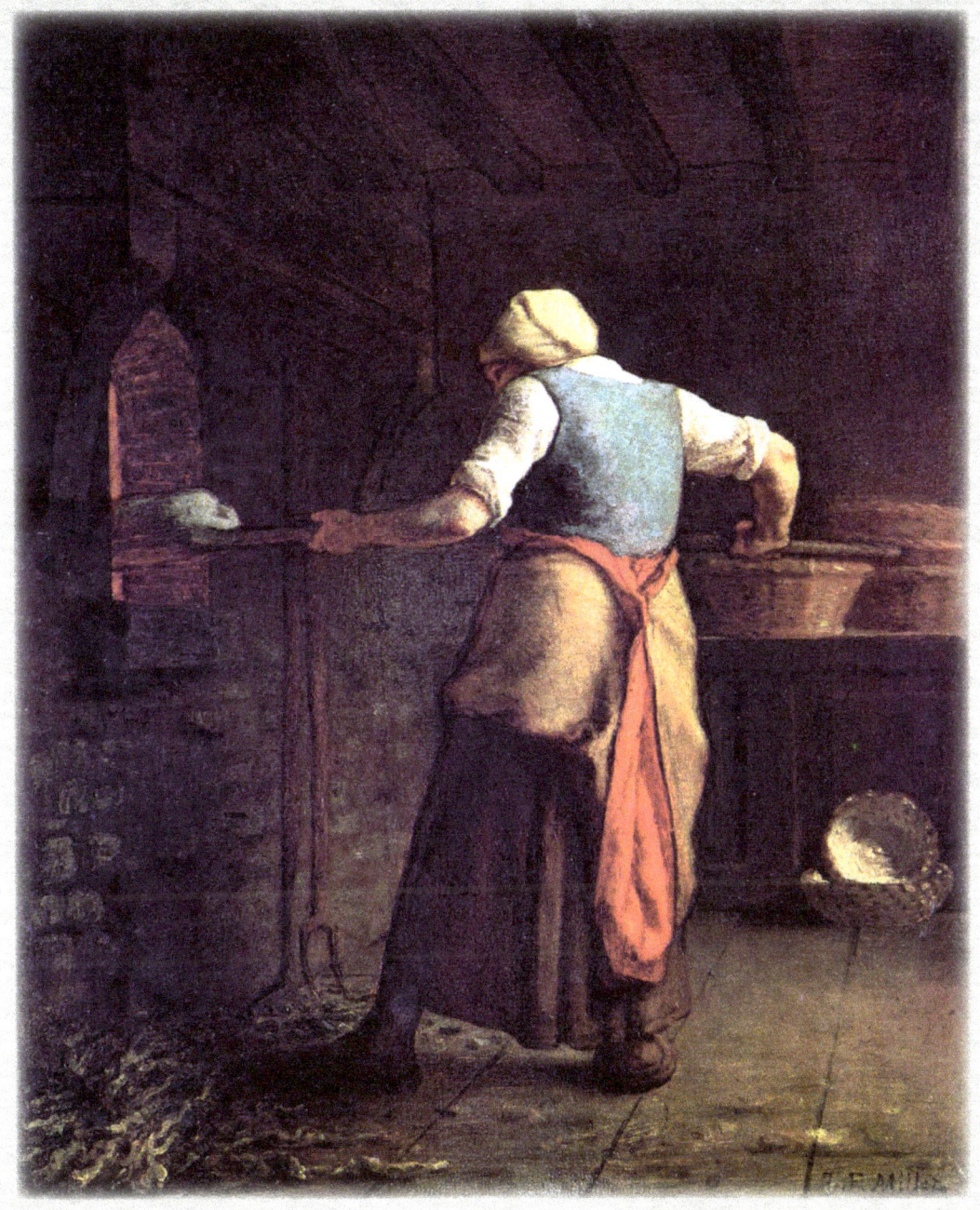

reflected light

See *shadow and light types.*

relief sculpture

a type of sculpture that is not free-standing but projects out from the surface it is carved or shaped from. When the sculpture projects out slightly, it is called *low relief* or *bas relief*. When it projects a great deal, it is called *high relief* or *haut relief*. From French *haut*, "high" and *bas*, "low" + Latin *relevo*, "to raise."

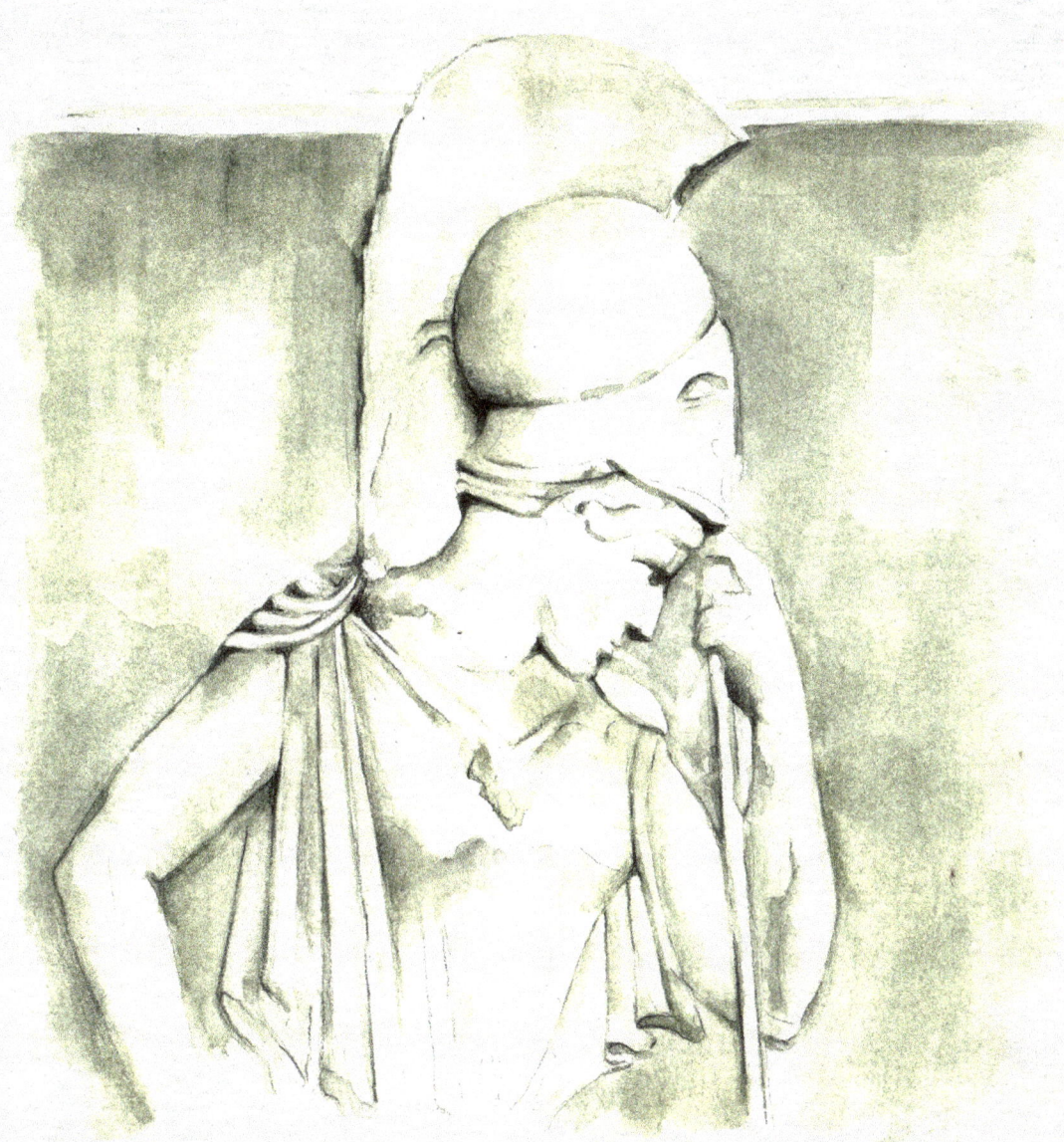

relief sculpture

Renaissance

one of the most important periods in the history of human culture. It began in Italy around 1400 and quickly spread throughout Europe. The beginning of the Renaissance marked the end of the Middle Ages, a time in Europe where earlier cultural, artistic and philosophical advances of the Greeks and Romans had been lost. During the Renaissance, these advances were reintroduced and a school of thought called Humanism emerged to become the leading philosophy of the time.

Humanism encouraged people to see their human capabilities, promoting education, beauty, and mastery of one's skills. An extraordinary time for the advancement of art and science, the Renaissance continued for about 200 years. Some of the most important figures of the Renaissance were the Italian artists Michelangelo, Leonardo da Vinci and Raphael. From French *renaissance*, "rebirth."

replica

an exact reproduction of an original work of art.

resin

a sculpting material that is lightweight and can be painted to look like stone or metal. There are natural resins that come from plants or insects and there are synthetic resins.

In painting, resin is a thick, transparent substance which can be mixed with paints or poured over a completed painting, hardening to a glossy finish.

romanticism

a movement starting in the late 1700s that emphasized the inspiration of nature, personal feelings, imagination and originality. It was a breaking away from the classical art traditions that had been revived in the Renaissance. Amongst a wide range of successful artists of this period were the English artists John Constable and William Blake (who was also a well-known poet), and the French artist Eugène Delacroix.

rule of thirds

a method of composition based on the concept that something placed off center is generally more pleasing than something placed right in the middle of an image. If one divides an image into thirds vertically and horizontally, where the lines cross can guide placement of key elements. These points are called *crash points* or *power points*. Additionally, dominant horizontal elements (such as horizon lines) or vertical elements (such as a tree or person) are often best placed along one of the horizontal or vertical lines. On the other hand, placing the dominant element of a piece or image in the center can create a strong feeling of power or stability, so this has its uses as well.

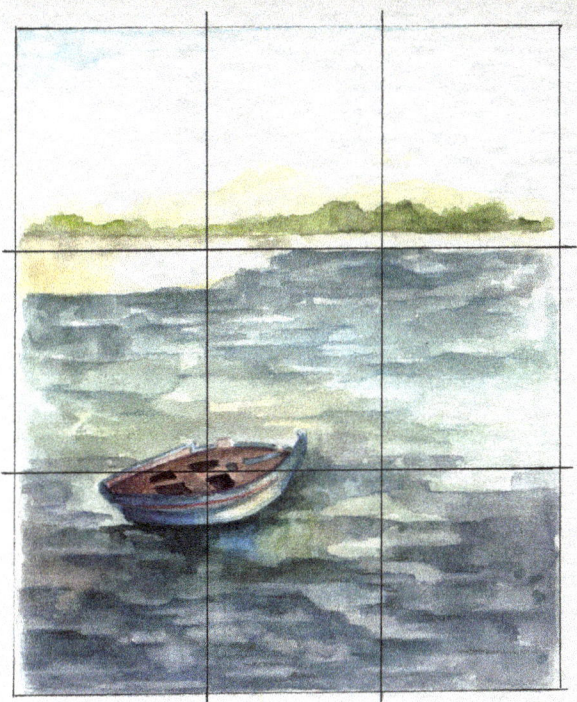

rule of thirds

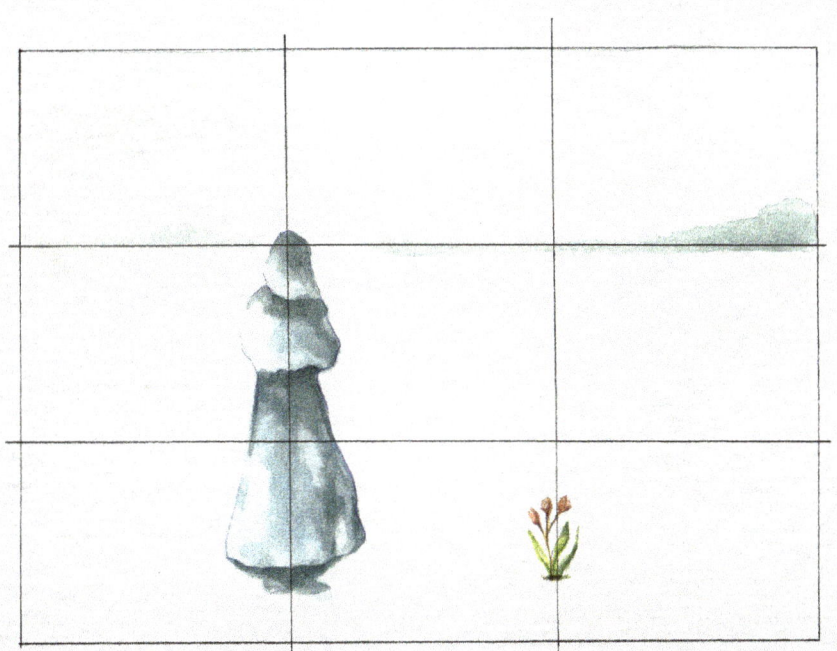

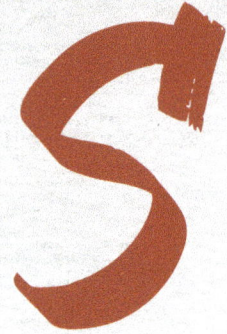

saturate

is to fill something completely so that no more can be added. For example, a sponge is saturated when it can hold no more liquid.

saturated

saturation

how vivid and pure a color is. A saturated image is bright and full of color whereas an unsaturated image is duller or grayer. In painting, desaturation—reducing the saturation—is usually achieved by adding white, black or gray to a color.

saturated

desaturated

scale

refers to the size of an object in relation to another object.
In experiencing the scale of a work of art, one tends to
compare its size to the size of one's own body.

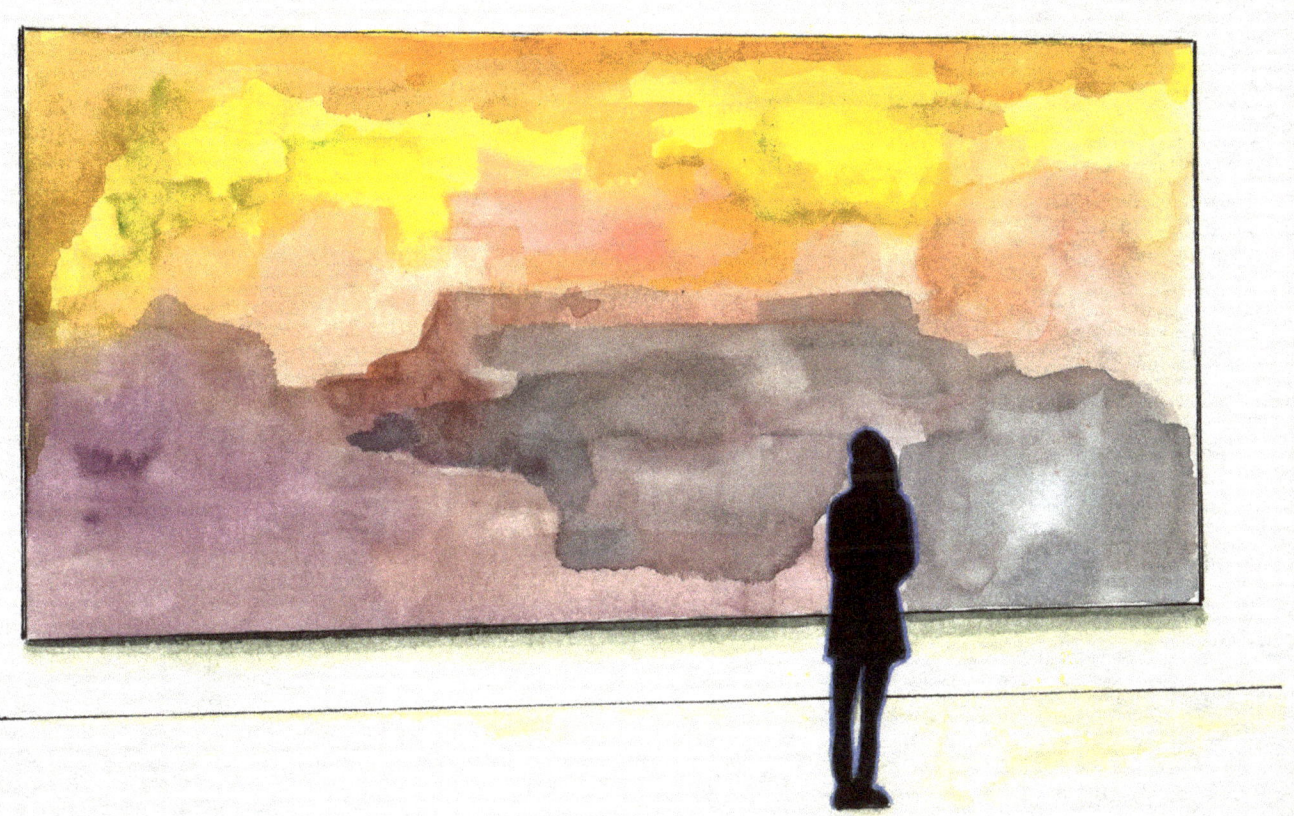

school

a group of artists sharing similar ideas, style or techniques. For examples given in this glossary, see *Barbizon school* and *Hudson River school*.

screen printing

or *silkscreen printing*

a traditional method of printing in which a stencil is placed on a screen of mesh-like material such as silk or nylon to which ink is applied. The ink is blocked by the stencil but penetrates the mesh, leaving an image on the paper, fabric or other surface receiving the ink. Multiple stencils can be used for multiple colors in making one print. This technique allows many prints to be made from one stencil or set of stencils.

scribble drawing

a drawing made with scribbles, or quick lines of any direction or size made without lifting the pen or pencil from the paper. Smaller, denser scribbles can be used for darker areas. Larger, more open scribbles can show lighter areas.

sculpture

three-dimensional art made of stone, wood, clay or any other material that can be shaped into a form. There are four basic methods of sculpting: carving, which takes away; modeling, which adds on; casting, which uses a mold; and constructing, which builds with one or more materials. From Latin *sculptura*, "a carving."

secondary colors

the three colors that result from mixing two primary colors:
violet (blue + red), green (blue + yellow) and orange (red + yellow).

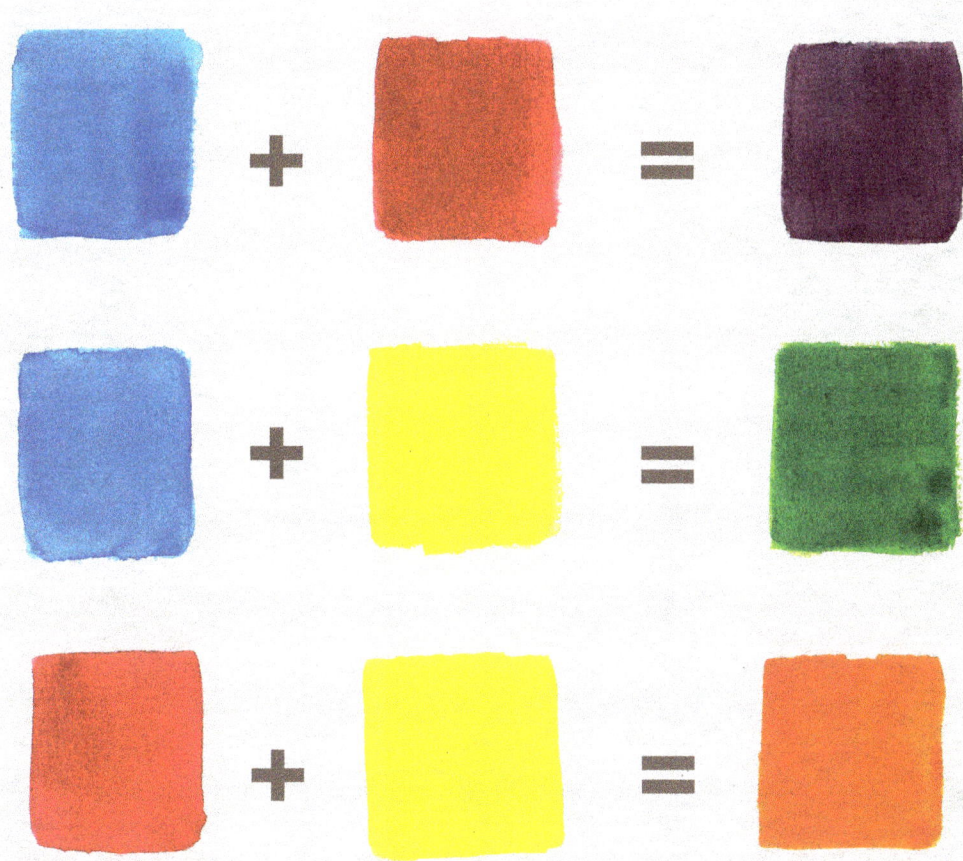

self-portrait

a painting, drawing, photograph or sculpture of an artist created by that artist.

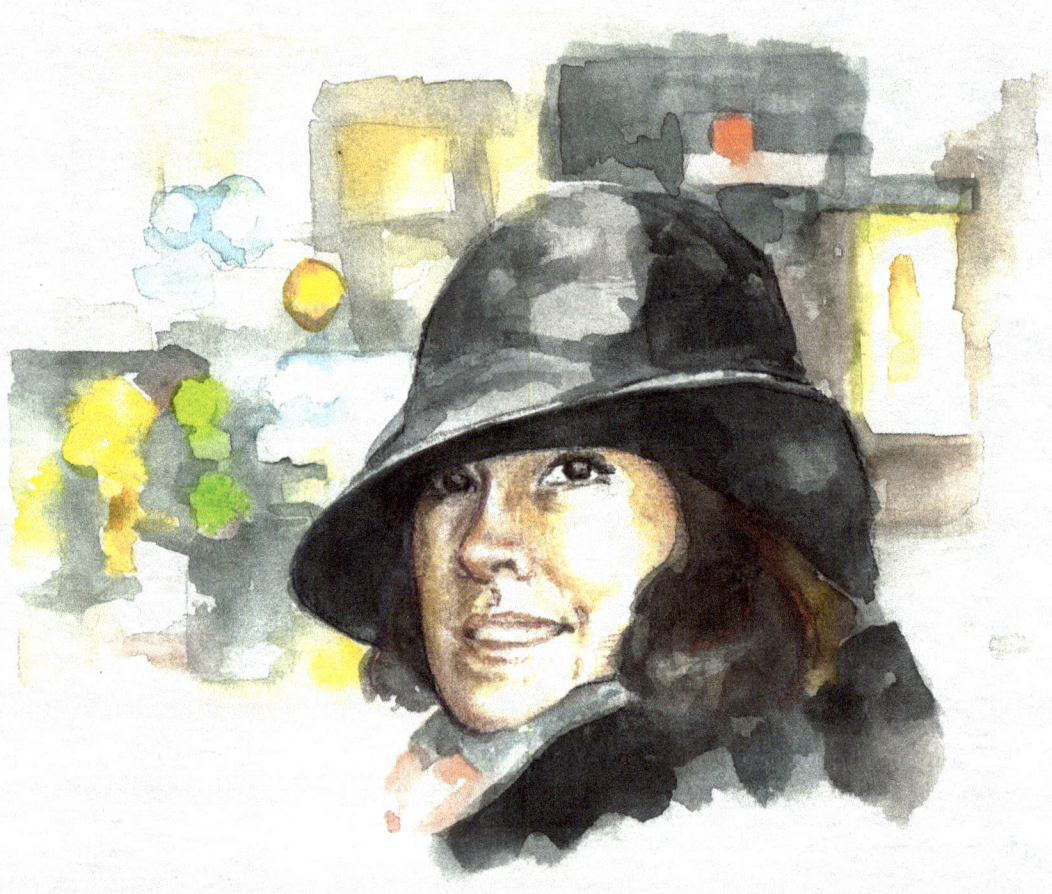

sfumato

a painting or drawing technique in which transitions from light to dark are softened so no specific line of change is visible. It creates a soft and natural effect in things like facial features or clouds. From Italian *sfumare*, "to evaporate."

shade

a shade of a color is the result of mixing any color with black.
A shade is darker than the original color. (Compare *tint* and *tone.*)

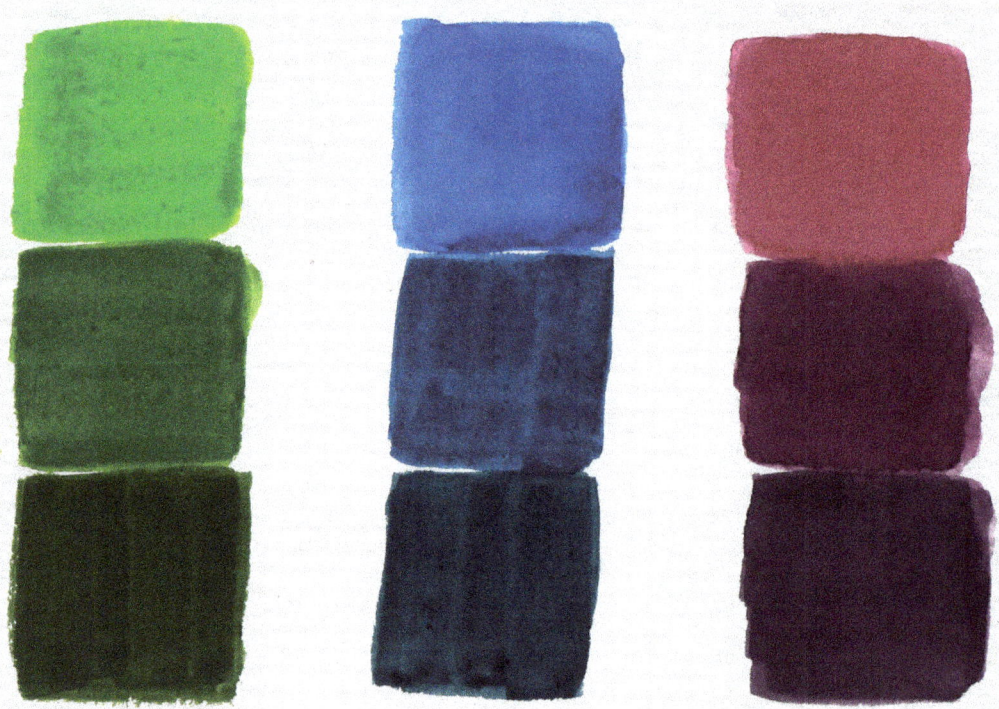

shading

the use of lines, color or denser pigment to darken or create the
illusion of shadows in a drawing or painting.

shadow and light types

there are names for different aspects of light and shadow on or near an object. The *core shadow* is the darkest shadow on the object itself. The shadow that falls onto the nearby surface is the *cast shadow*. The darkest section of shadow off the object is the *occlusion shadow*.

On the lighted side of the object there is the *core light* or *direct light*. Next to this is the *mid tone*. The lightest value, usually white, is a reflection of light called the *highlight*. On the shadow side, some light normally bounces off the surface on which the object sits, making that part a little lighter. This is called *reflected light*.

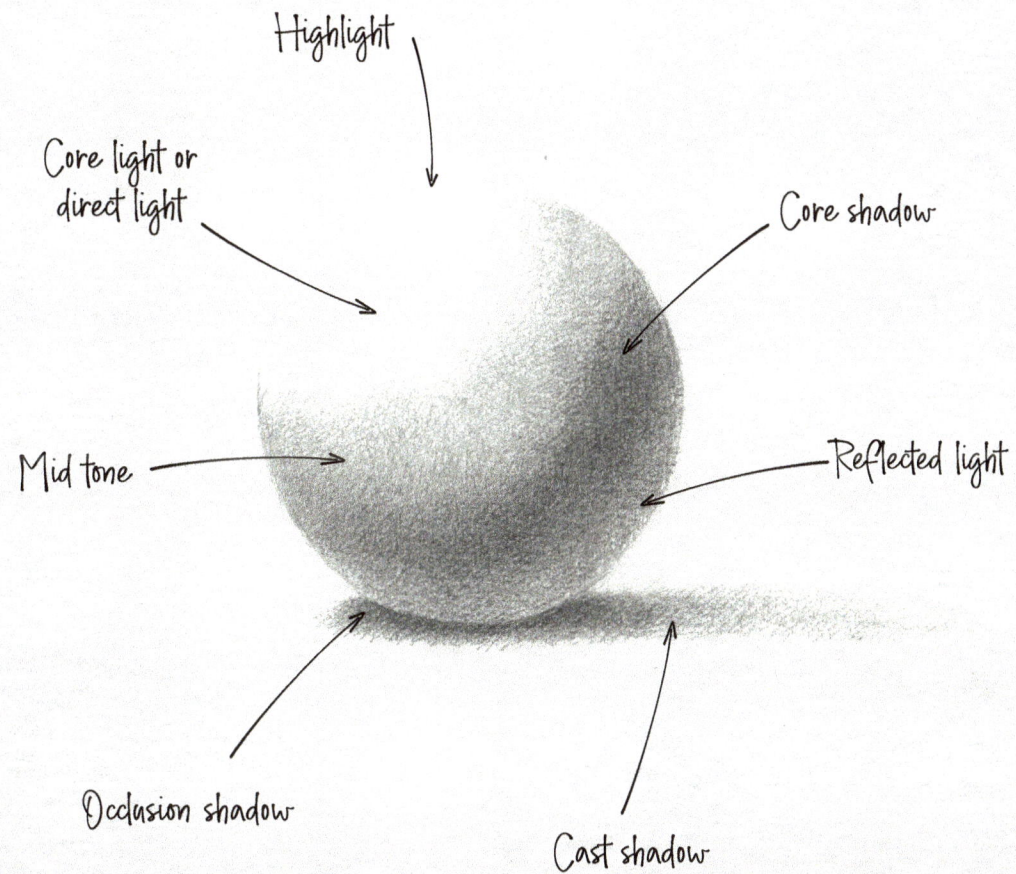

Highlight

Core light or direct light

Core shadow

Mid tone

Reflected light

Occlusion shadow

Cast shadow

shape

an enclosed space made by making a line come all the way back to its starting point. Shapes are the basic building blocks of any drawing or painting. (See *geometric shape* and *organic shape.*)

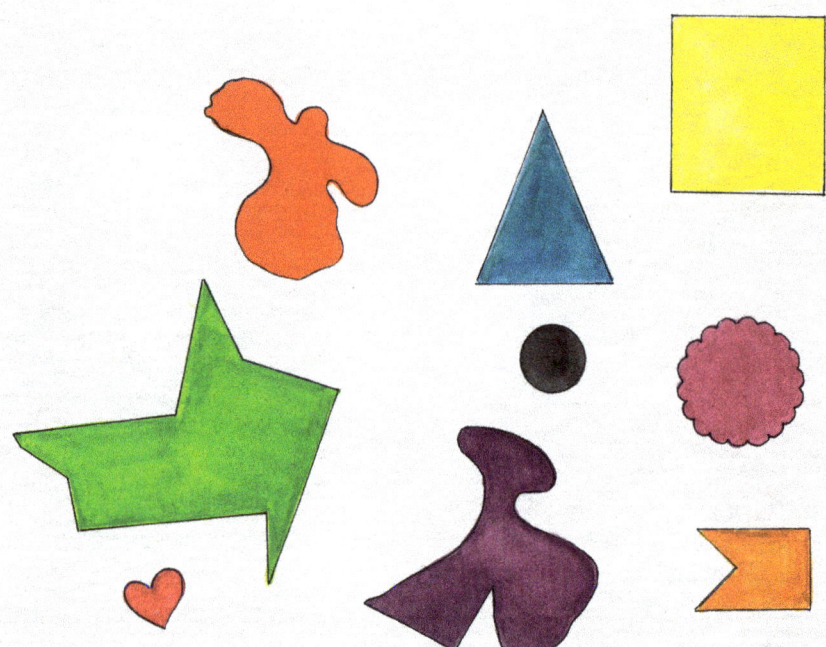

silhouette

the dark shape and outline of someone or something in front of a lighter background.

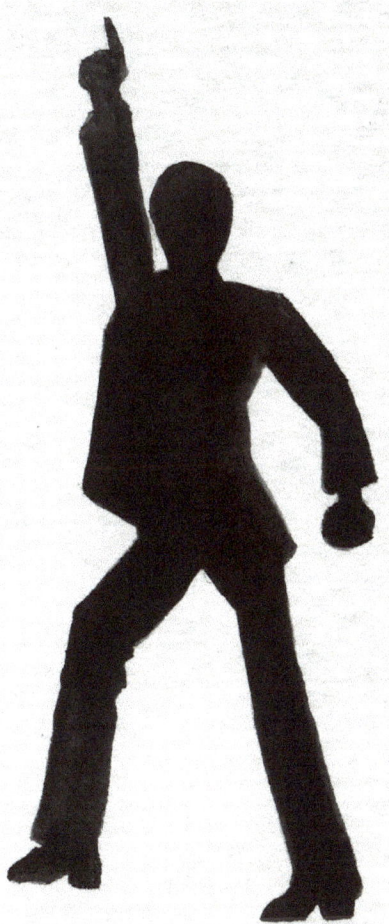

simulated texture

texture that is not actual but an illusion, such as a drawing or painting showing the softness of a velvet dress, the jagged edges of a rock or the roughness of a tree trunk. (Compare *real texture.*)

sketch

a rapidly executed drawing, frequently done for practice or as preparation for a more developed work.

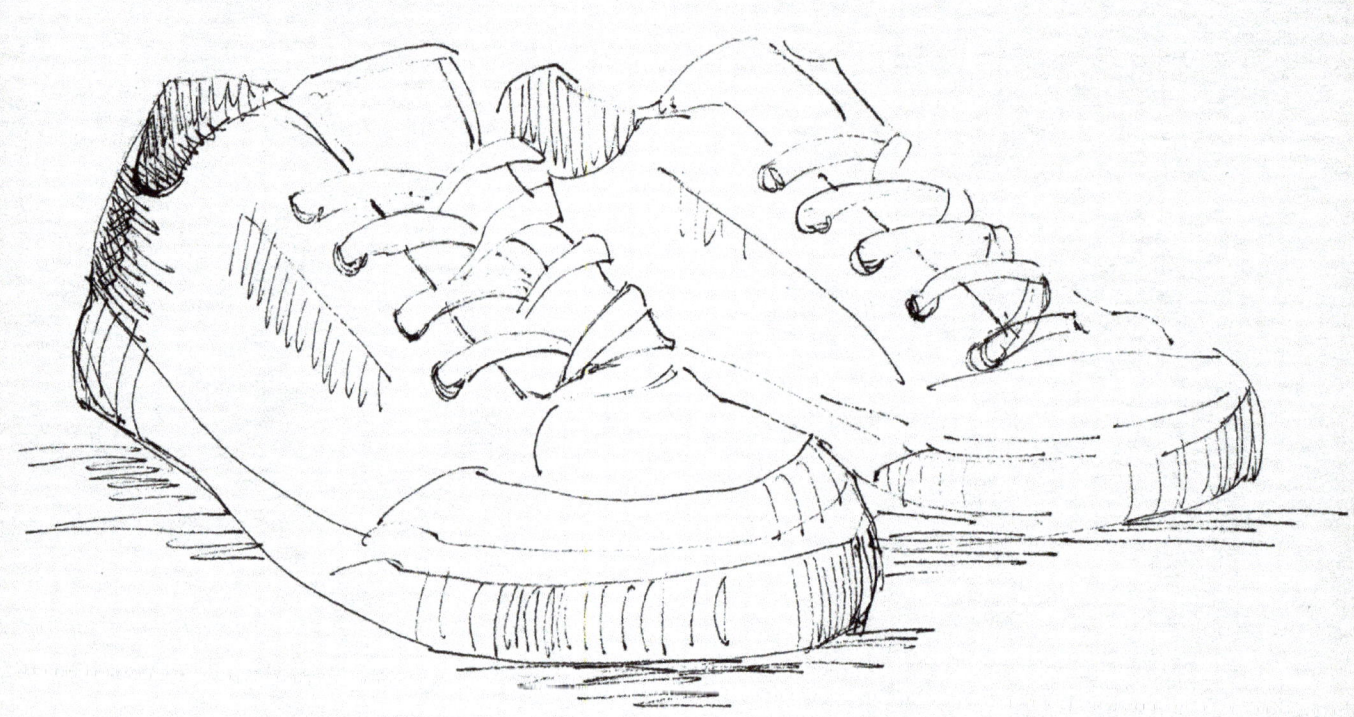

soapstone

a type of soft stone used in sculpture. Though soft, it can be found in varying degrees of hardness. Soapstone has been used for thousands of years in carving both artistic and practical pieces.

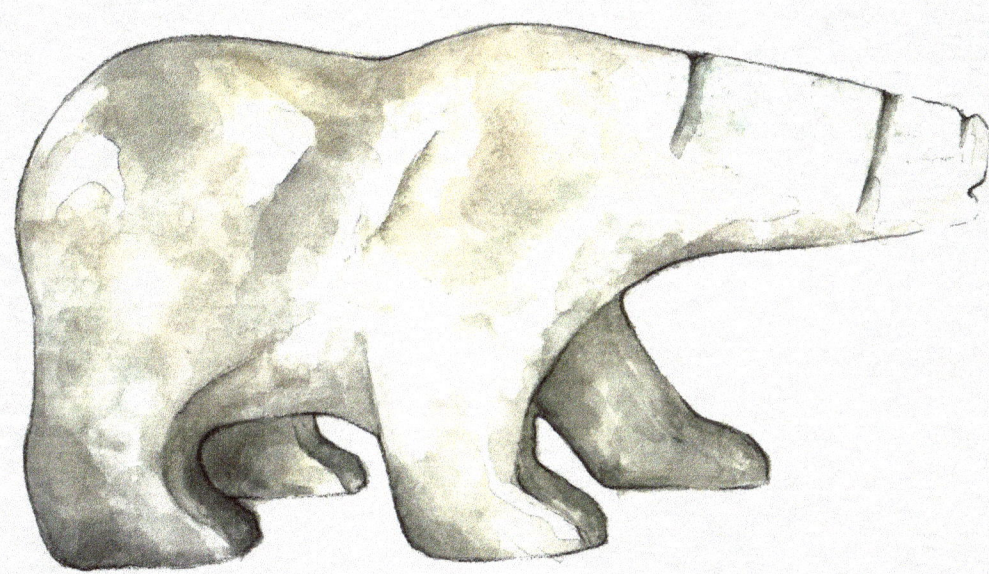

spike lavender

an oil taken from a particular variety of the lavender plant sometimes used as a solvent for oil paint. (See *turpentine.*)

statue

a sculpture of a person or animal, normally life-size or larger.

still life painting

a painting of objects arranged together. It is called still life because it can include anything which does not move, such as flowers or even dead animals.

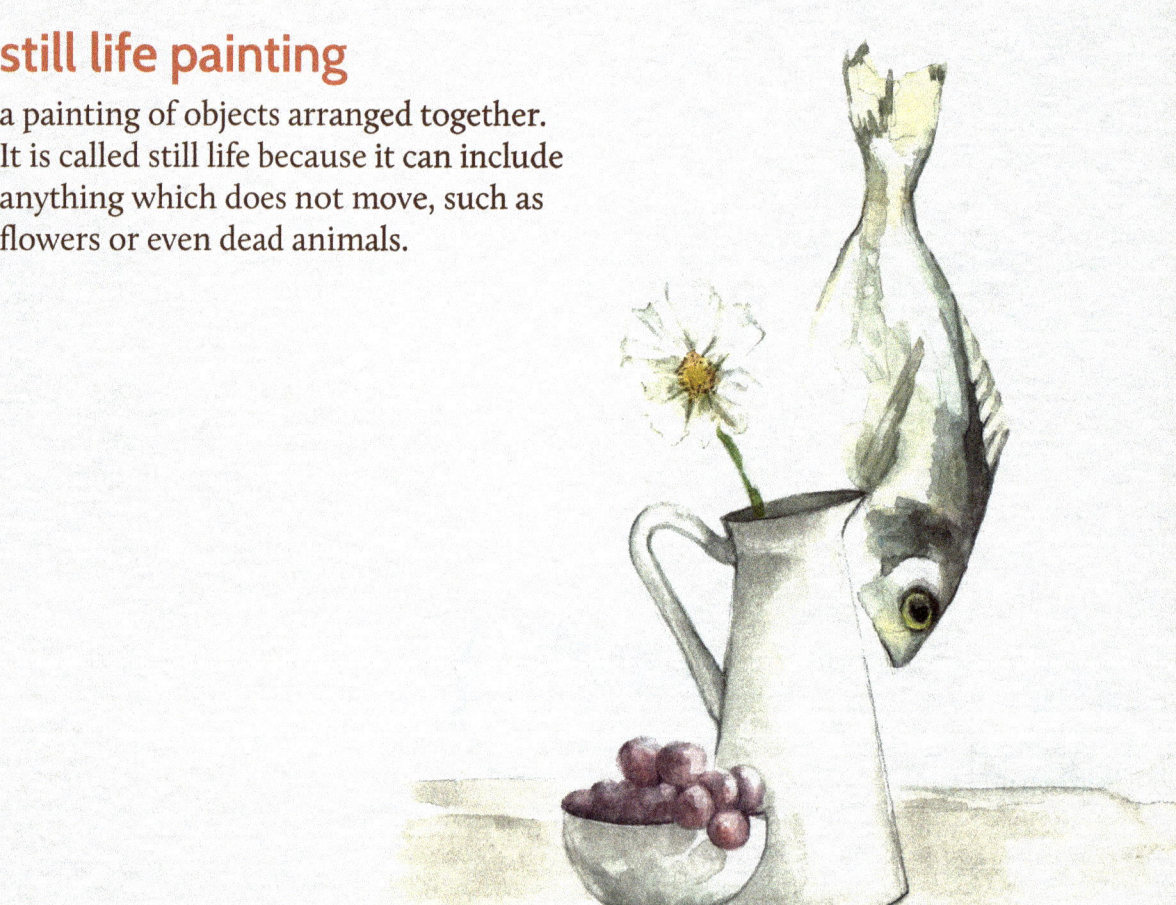

stippling

a drawing technique that uses many small dots to construct or shade an image.

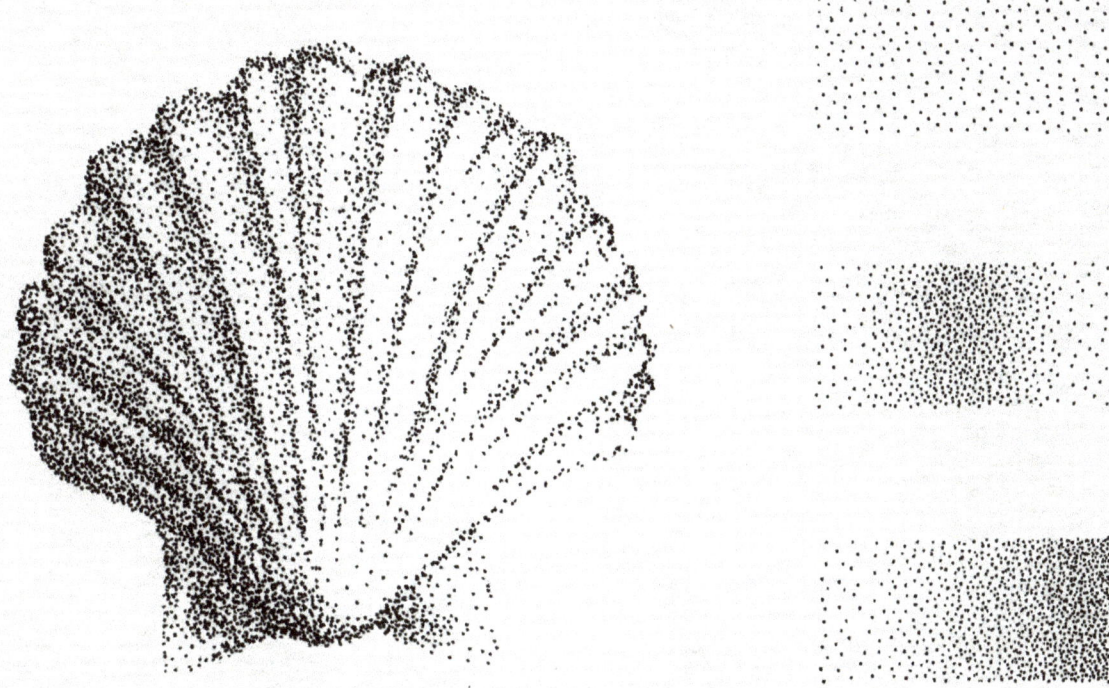

stoneware

a type of thick, hard, clay pottery baked at a high temperature, making it resistant to liquids. Because of its liquid-resistant and durable, stone-like qualities, stoneware is often used for food-serving items such as cups, plates and bowls.

stretcher

a wooden, frame-like structure to which one fixes a fabric such as canvas, stretching it tight so it can be painted on.

studio

a room in which an artist or sculptor works.

stylus

a pen-shaped device used in digital art which acts as a drawing or writing tool on a screen. Also, a pointed instrument made of metal, bone or wood used in ancient times to write on wax.

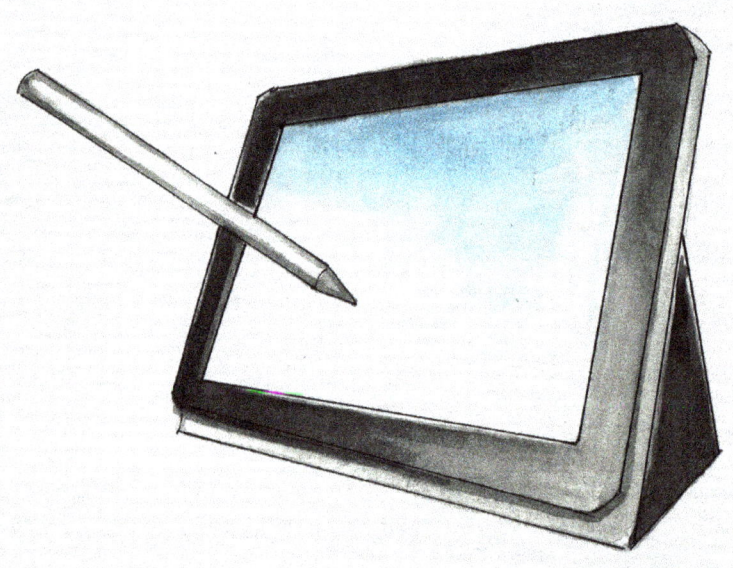

support

the surface on which a painting is made, such as paper, canvas, wood or metal.

surrealism

an art movement begun in the 1920s that was inspired by dreams, the unconscious mind, poetry and imagination. Surrealism means "beyond reality." Some of the most famous surrealists were the Spanish painter Salvador Dalí, the Belgian painter René Magritte, and the German painter Max Ernst.

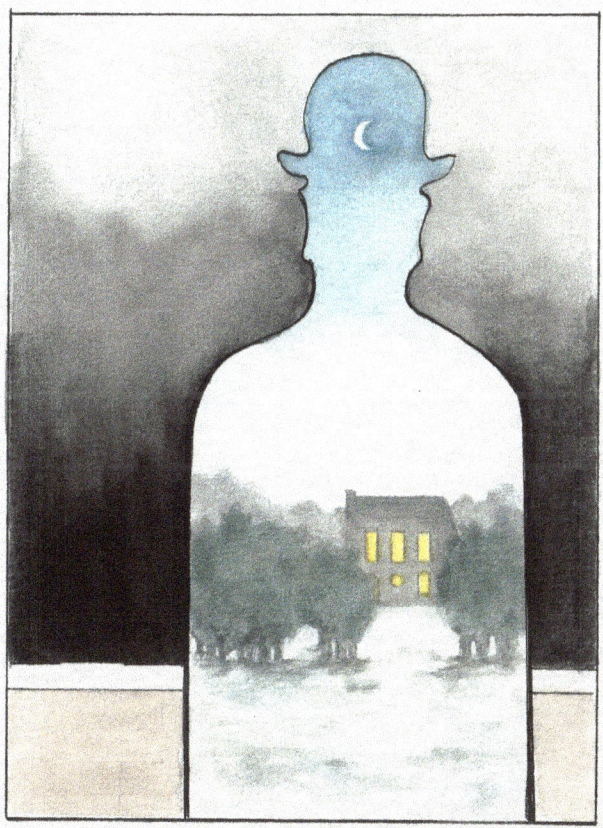

symmetry

a quality where two sides of something are the same or similar, or feel balanced. In art, it describes the elements of a composition feeling or appearing in balance, whether in size, shape or color, creating a pleasing feeling for the viewer.

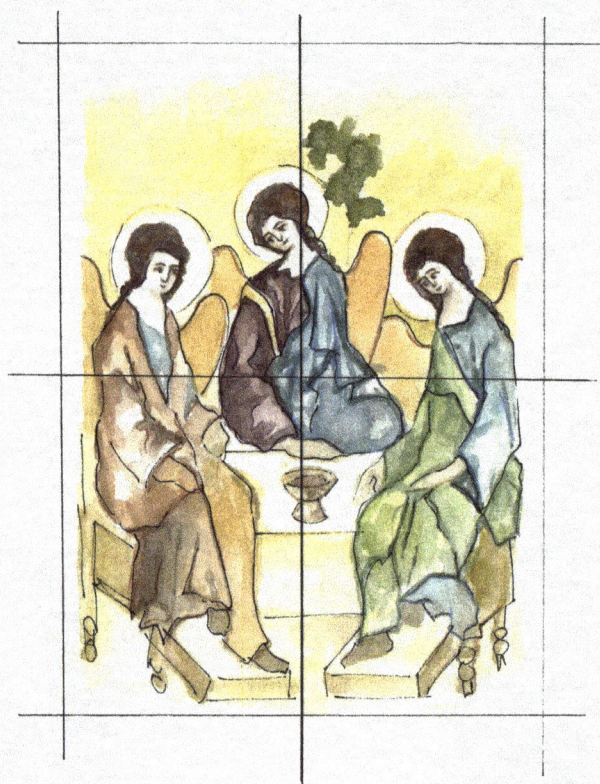

synthetic

made artificially, not from natural materials. For example, paintbrush bristles can be made from a natural material like hog's hair or a synthetic material like nylon.

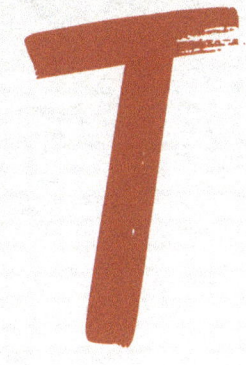

tapestry

a piece of heavy fabric with artwork woven into it, often used as a wall hanging. From French *tapis*, "heavy fabric" or "carpet."

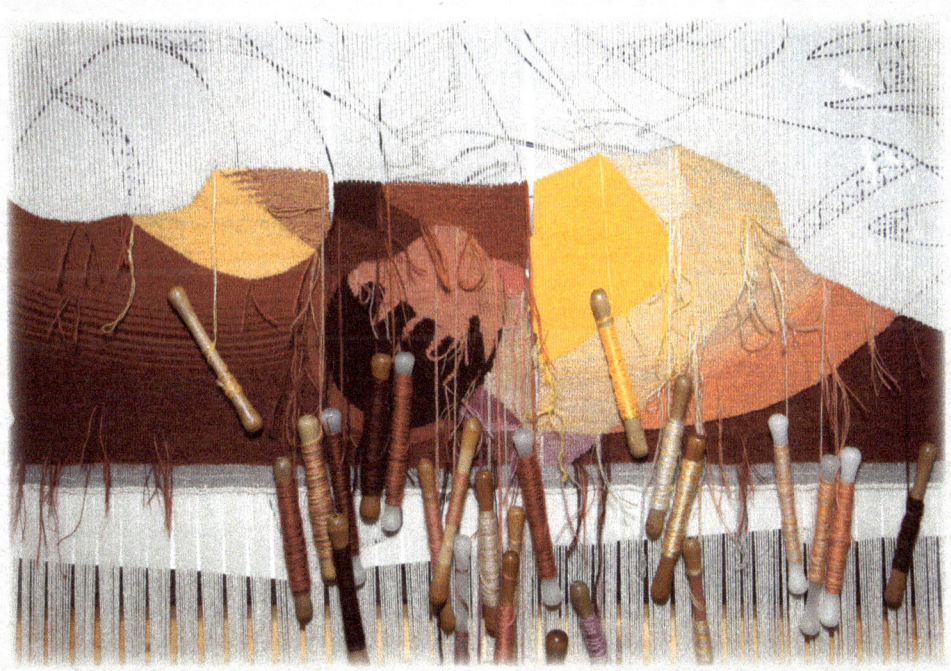

technique

a precise method of doing something. Every art form has many techniques. Part of learning an art form is learning how different effects are created with different techniques. Mastering the variety of techniques in an art form enables an artist to utilize creativity and imagination to full effect.

tempera

a painting medium that was widely used before oil paints were developed. Tempera paint is made by mixing color pigments with water and eggs, and sometimes glue and milk as well. It was used widely in the 1300s and 1400s. Some artists still use it today.

tertiary colors

when two primary colors (red, yellow, blue) are mixed, secondary colors (orange, green, violet) result. On a color wheel, the six colors between these primary and secondary colors are called tertiary colors. Examples are red-orange, yellow-orange and blue-green. (*Primary* means first, *secondary* means second, *tertiary* means third.)

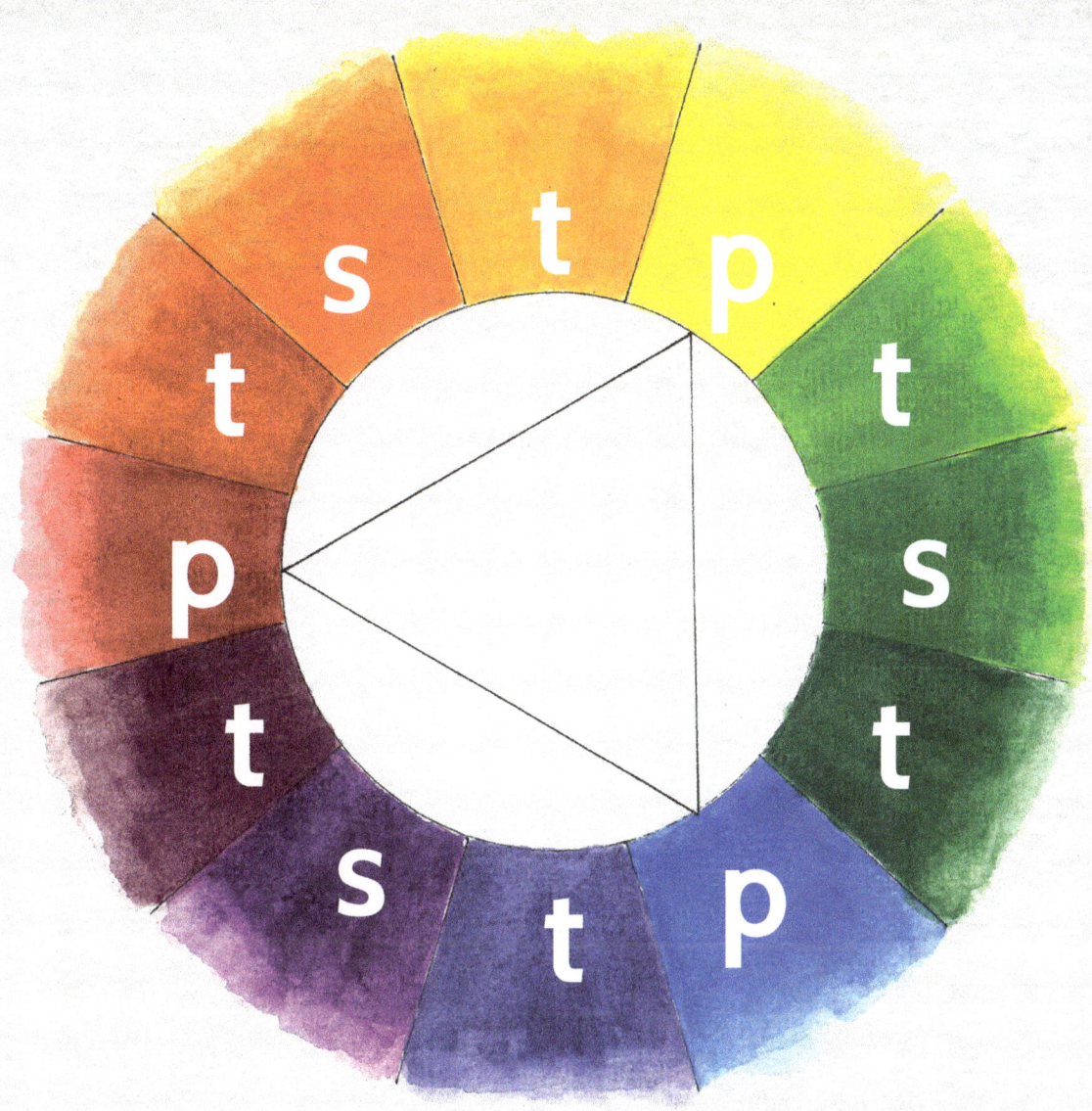

p: primary
s: secondary
t: tertiary

textile art

textiles are types of cloth or woven fabric, whether from plant, animal or human-made fibers. Textile art is art or crafts made by weaving, sewing, embroidering or gluing a variety of textiles, threads or yarn together.

texture

the surface quality of a work of art, such as its smoothness or roughness and how it appears it would feel. Texture can be both seen with the eyes and felt through the sense of touch. (See *real texture* and *simulated texture*.)

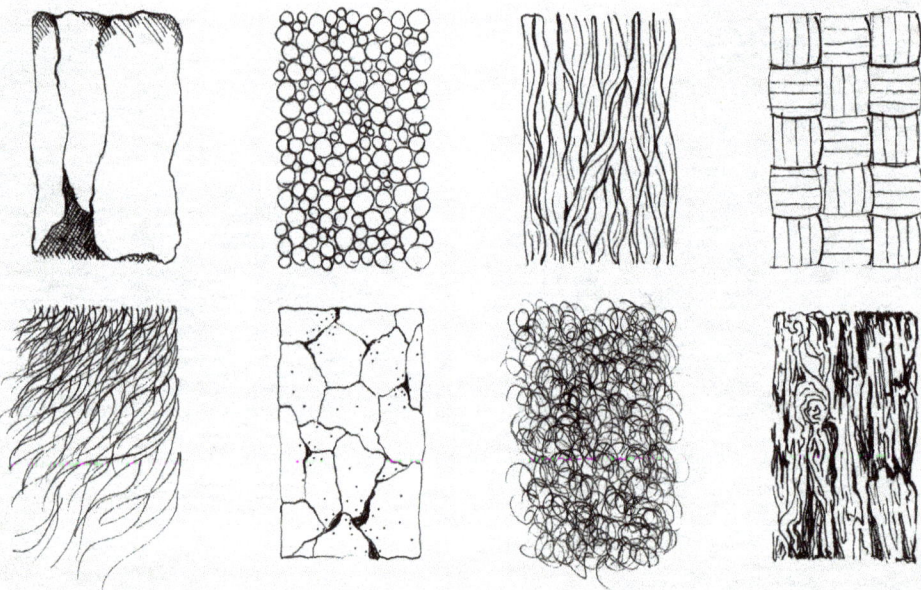

three-dimensional

anything that has three measurable dimensions, length, width and height, as opposed to something flat, which has only two dimensions.

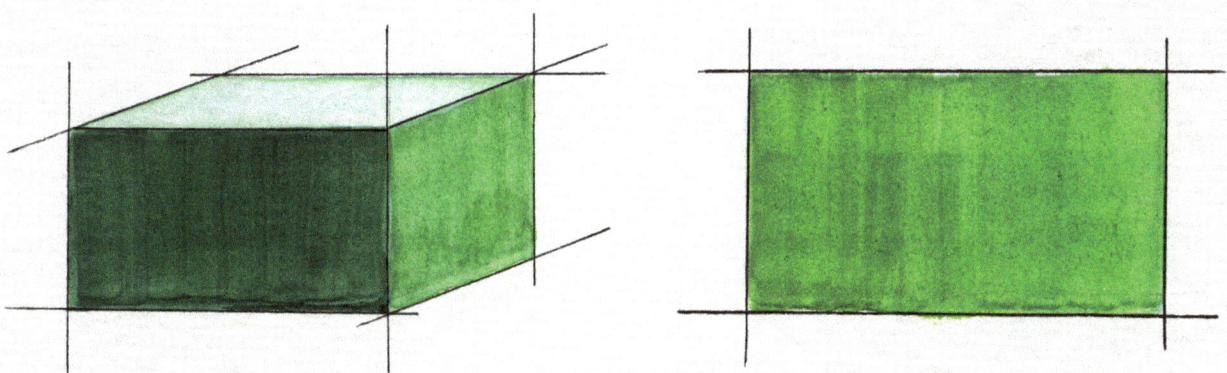

three-point perspective

a technique for creating perspective that uses two vanishing points on the horizon and a third vanishing point that is below the ground or in the sky. This has particular use in drawing buildings from a viewpoint above. (Compare *one-point perspective* and *two-point perspective.*)

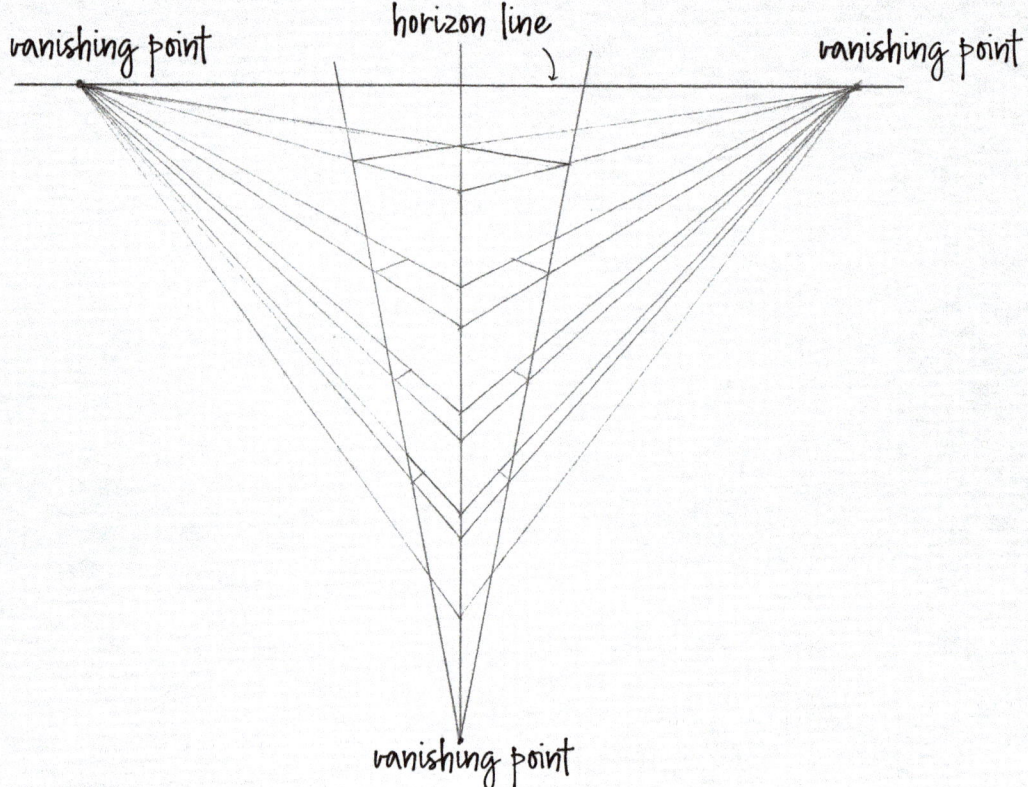

throw

to form (a ceramic piece) on a pottery wheel.

tilt line

See *center axis.*

tint

a tint is the result of mixing a color with white. What we normally call "pastel" colors, which are soft and light, are actually tints of darker, richer or more vibrant colors. In watercolor, a tint is achieved with a thinner layer of color that allows the white of the paper to show through. (Compare *shade* and *tone.*)

tone

different *tones* of a color are produced by adding gray (black and white), which reduces the purity of a color. (Compare *tint* and *shade.*)

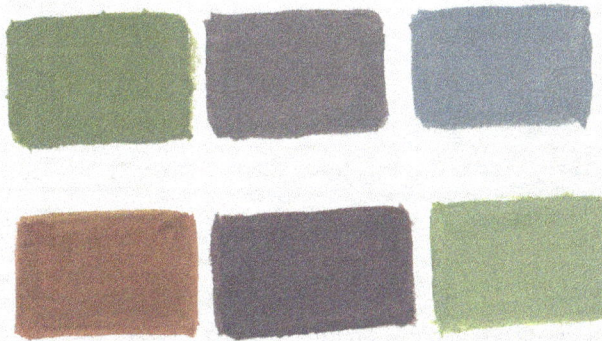

tooth

the texture of a paper, canvas or any surface which helps to
hold the paint. The greater the texture, the more holding
power and therefore the more "tooth."

transparency

the degree to which you can see through something.
(Compare *opacity.*)

trompe l'oeil (trohmp-loy)

a painting that deceives the eye by creating an exact illusion of a real object or person. An example would be a painting of a garden at the end of a hallway, which creates a feeling of being outdoors. From French *trompe*, "trick or deceive" + *l'oeil*, "the eye."

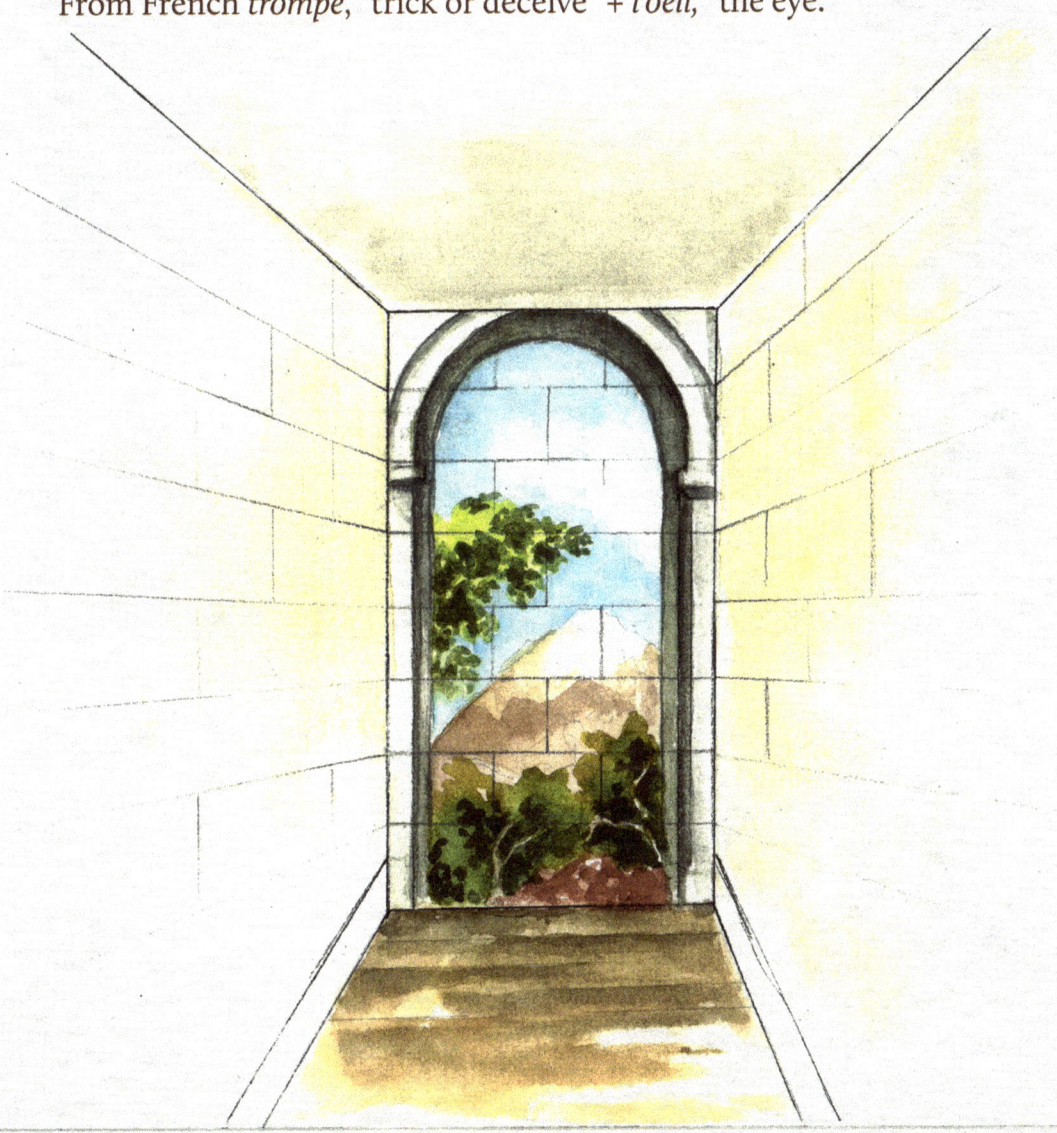

triptych (trip tick)

a work of art consisting of three separate pieces that are meant to go together. (Compare *diptych*.)

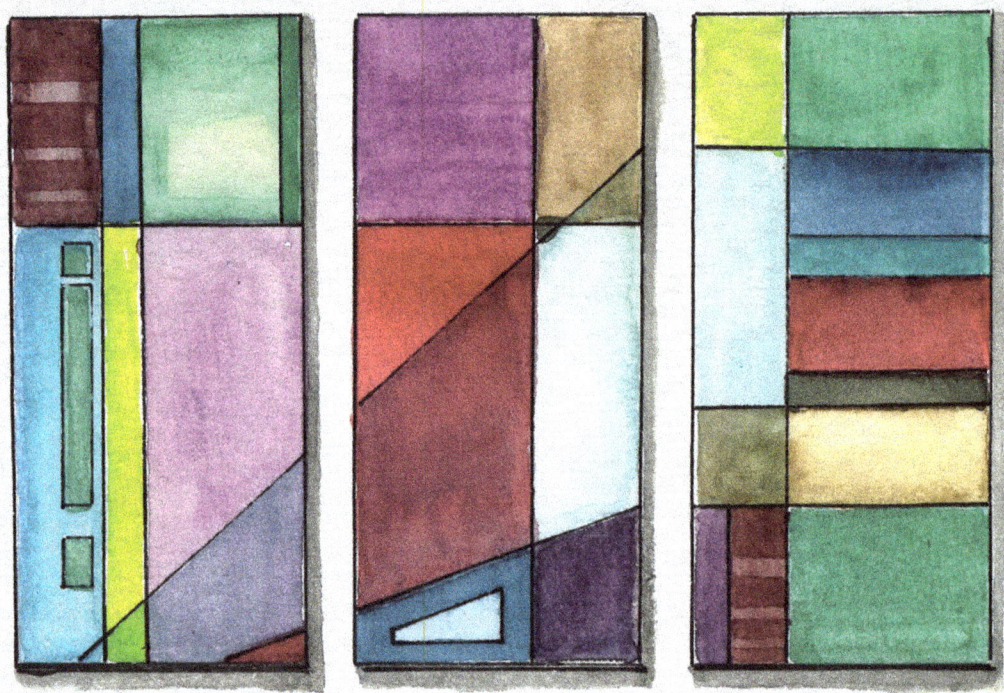

turpentine

a liquid used as a solvent in cleaning oil paint from brushes and other painting supplies. Mixed with linseed oil, it makes a lighter medium for oil paint than linseed oil alone. Turpentine and similar solvents can be irritants, so in its place some artists use spike lavender, an oil from a particular variety of lavender plant. In using turpentine, precautions should be taken to limit fumes and protect the skin.

two-point perspective

a technique for creating perspective that uses two vanishing points on the horizon. It has many applications in drawing and painting. It can be used, for example, to draw geometric objects or street scenes viewed from an angle, diverging roads lined with trees, and much more. (Compare *one-point perspective* and *three-point perspective*.)

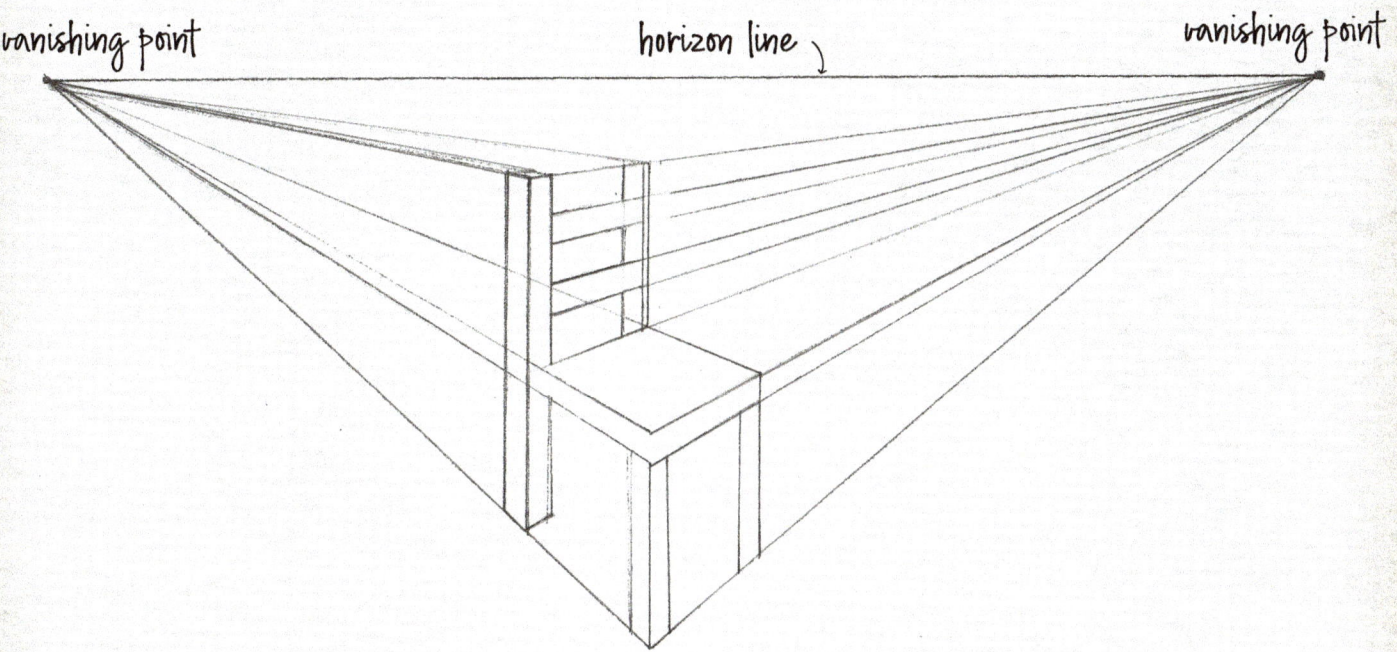

vanishing point

horizon line

vanishing point

typography

the art of arranging type so that what is written is readable and engaging.

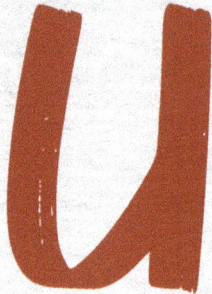

underdrawing

a sketch made by an artist on the paper or canvas to be used as a guide before applying paint or ink.

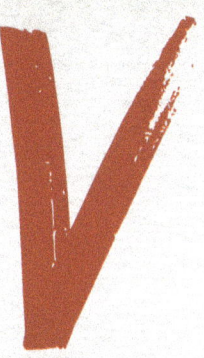

value

the lightness or darkness of a color. It is also the relationship
between the lights and darks in a work of art. For example,
there can be gradual or sudden transitions from light
to dark elements, there can be strong
contrasts between light and dark
elements, or there can be dominant
light or dark values in a piece.

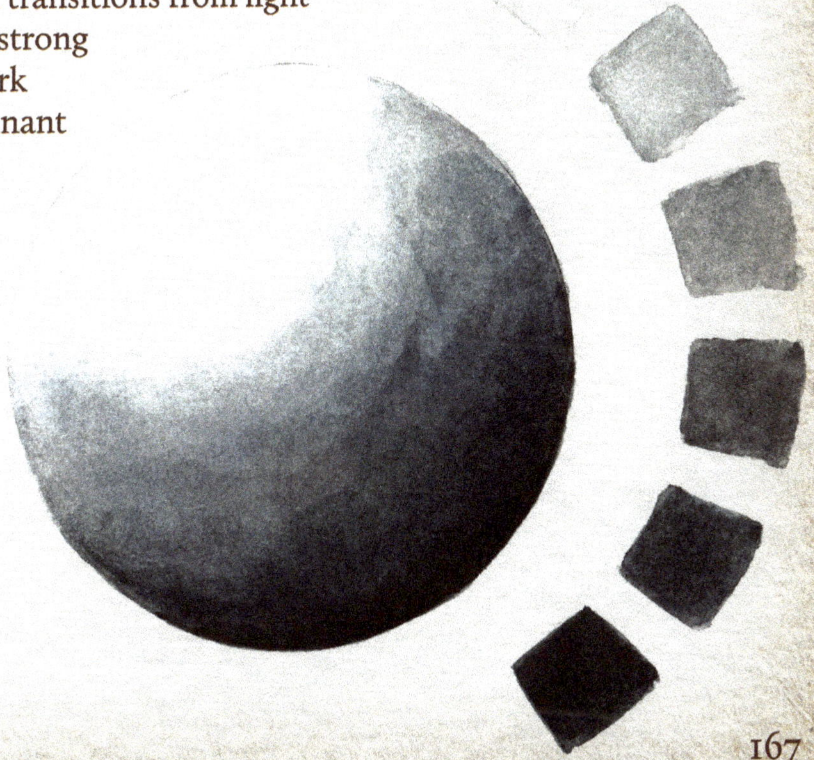

value scale

a system of gradually darker shades, from white to black. It can have only a few shades of gray or many. The value scale shown here has eight different values from white to black.

value transition

how values transition (change) from light to dark or dark to light. Objects like boxes, chairs and buildings have sharp edges and are more likely to show sudden changes in value. Representations of softer objects such as clothes, faces or clouds will tend to have more gradual changes from dark to light.

vanishing point

in perspective drawing, the vanishing point is an imaginary spot where objects in the distant horizon seem to converge and disappear. (See *one-point perspective*, *two-point perspective* and *three-point perspective*.)

varnish

a transparent, protective layer applied on a surface or artwork as the last step of the painting or drawing process.

video art

art which is made using video and audio recordings
and projections.

vignette (vin yet)

a small, unbordered illustration where the outer edges gradually
fade into the paper or surface on which it is made, often used in
portraits. Also, any illustration or decorative element in a book,
such as vine leaves used as a border. From French *vigne*,
"little vine."

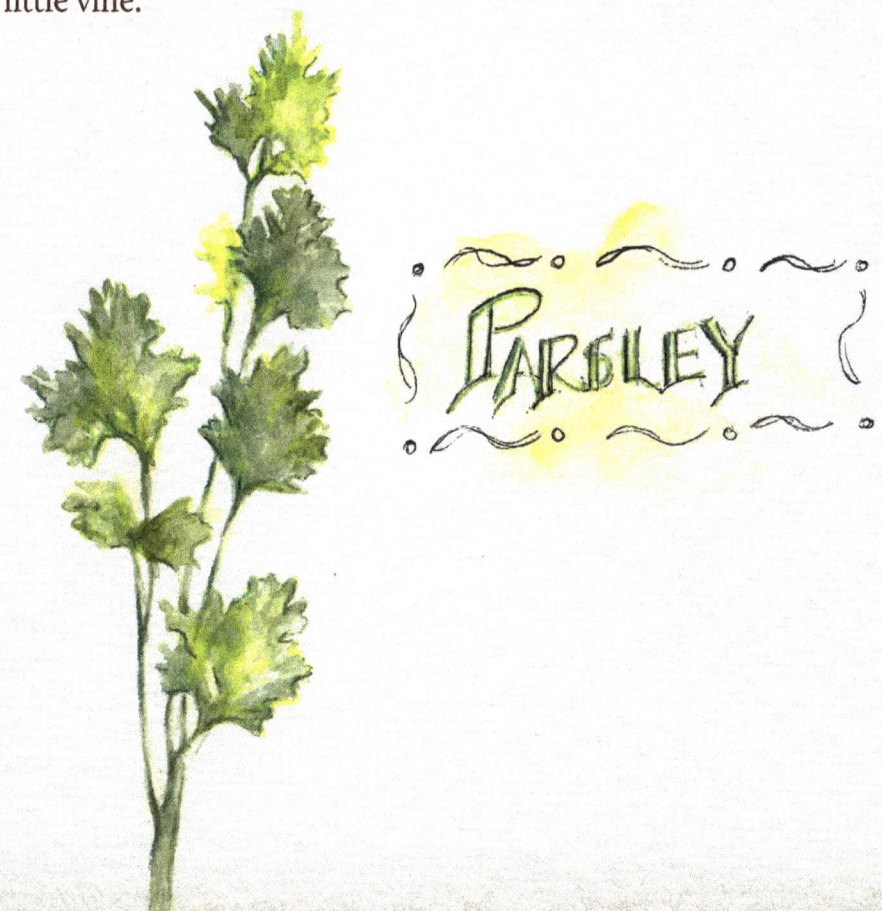

PARSLEY

vine charcoal

a type of drawing charcoal made from thin twigs of grape vines. It produces a dark gray color.

visual arts

a broad zone of art forms, normally thought of as including drawing, painting, printmaking, ceramics, sculpture, photography, film, architecture and crafts.

visual hierarchy

hierarchy generally refers to the arrangement of persons or things according to rank or importance. The visual hierarchy of an art piece refers to the arrangement or presentation of elements in a way that implies importance. From Greek *hieros*, "sacred" + *arkhes*, "ruler."

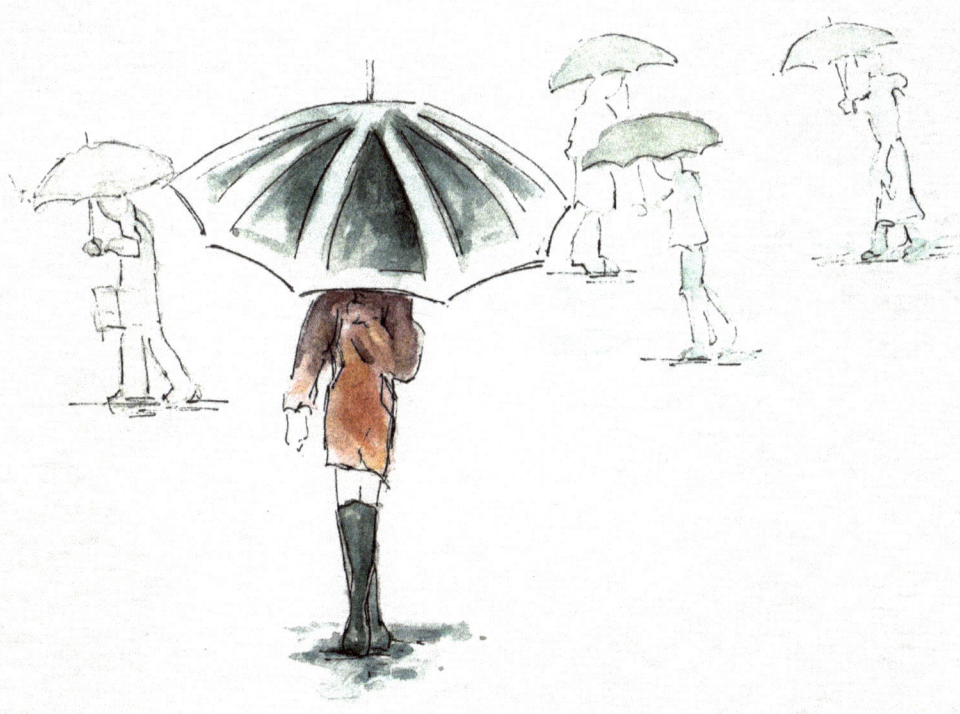

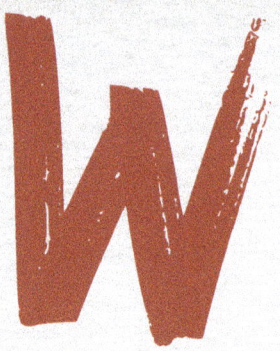

warm

colors that have red or yellow in them are often called warm. This comes from the observation that natural things that are warm or hot, such as sunlight or fire, tend to look red or yellow. (Compare *cool.*)

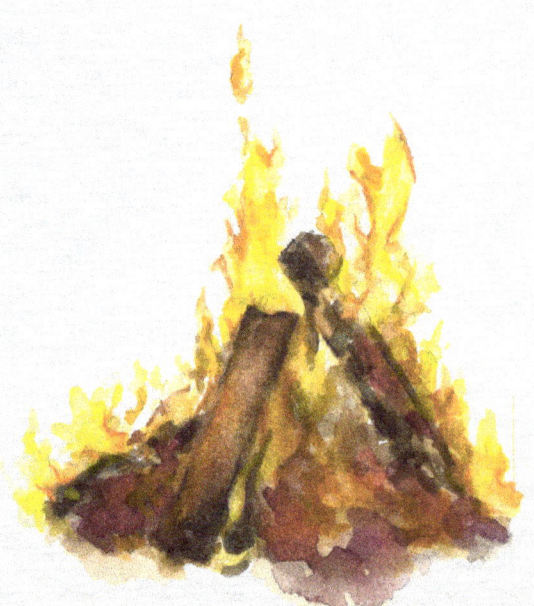

wash

or *glaze*

a thin, transparent layer of paint applied over an earlier layer to slightly alter or enhance its colors and create depth. A wash can be made with diluted watercolor, oil or acrylic paint.

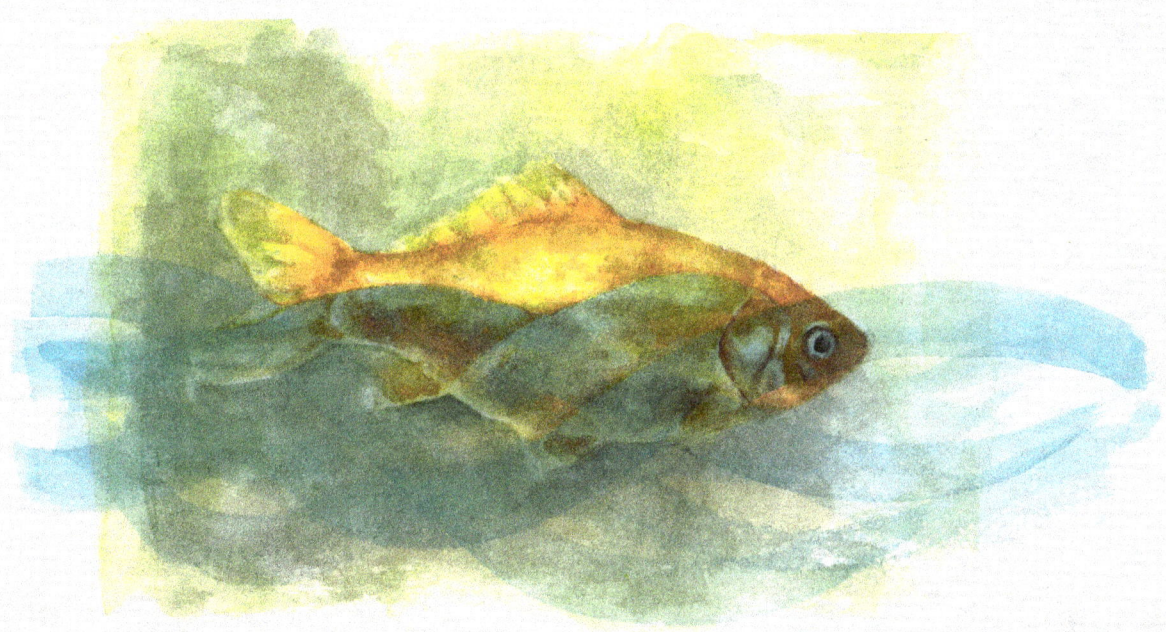

watercolor

a type of paint that dissolves with water. This kind of paint is more transparent and uses the lightness or whiteness of paper for its lighter colors and whites.

wheel

See *pottery wheel.*

wood carving

making objects or sculptures out of wood by cutting with tools like knives, gouges and chisels.

woodcut print

a printmaking technique that uses an image carved in wood
(called a *wood block*) that is inked and used to make prints.

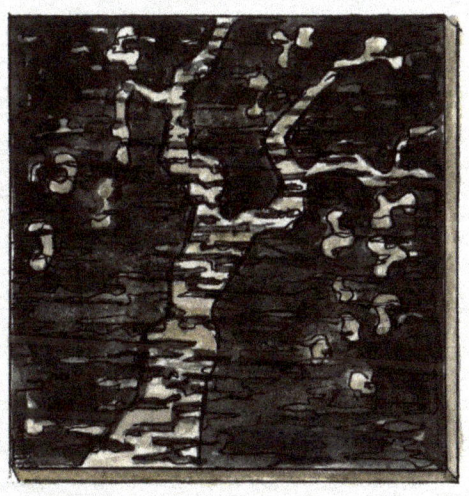

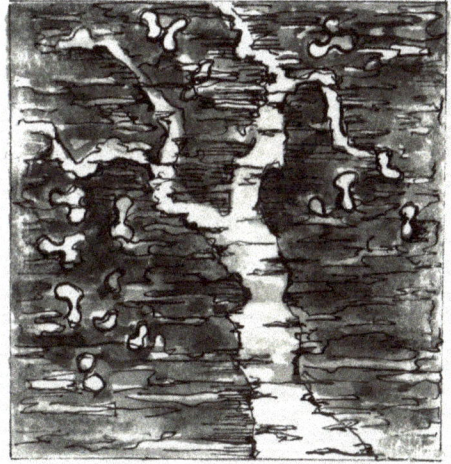

A TIMELINE OF
PERIODS, MOVEMENTS AND STYLES

Using the periods, movements and styles defined in this glossary, here is an overview of the history of visual arts in western culture. Though only labels representing approximations on a timeline, they can encourage exploration of knowledge and techniques useful in improving one's art.

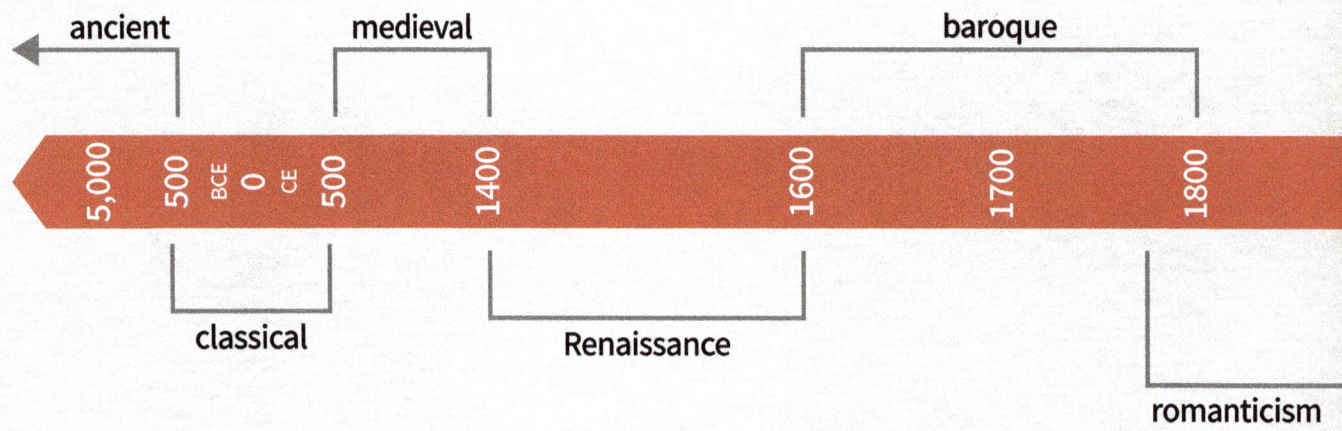

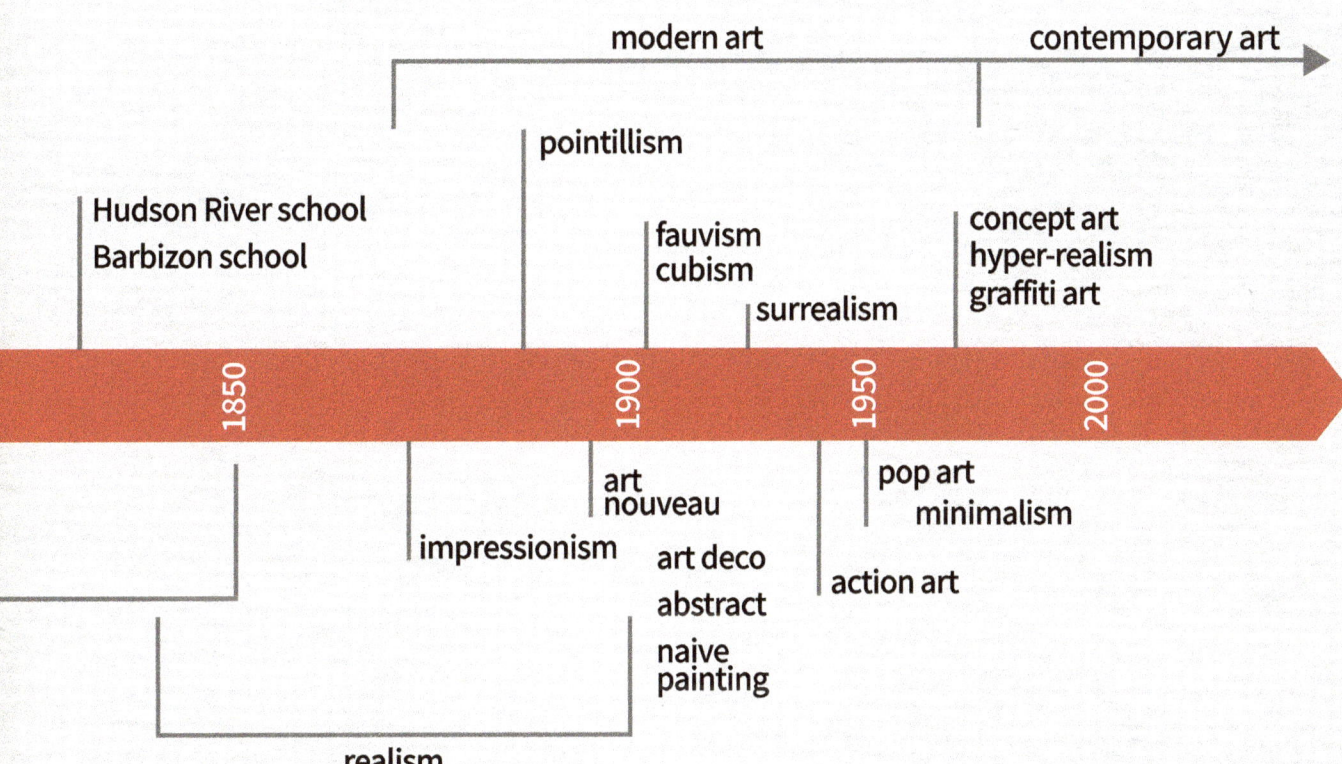

modern art

contemporary art

pointillism

Hudson River school
Barbizon school

fauvism
cubism

concept art
hyper-realism
graffiti art

surrealism

1850

1900

1950

2000

art
nouveau

impressionism

pop art
minimalism

art deco
abstract

action art

naive
painting

realism

ABOUT NATASHA

An internationally exhibited artist, teacher and curriculum designer, Natasha Gray was born in 1969 in Mexico City. After completing middle and high school at the Delphian School in Oregon, which she credits with "opening my eyes to the wonders and beauty of study and learning," she went on to study fine arts at the Academia de San Carlos, the Art Students League of New York and the School of Visual Art in Paris. While in New York she worked under renowned Spanish artist Miguel Angel Argüello (1941–2005).

What followed was an eight-year pilgrimage into the ghost towns and deserts of the Southwest U.S. With only a small camper and paint supplies, she set aside all modern comforts to focus herself on studies of light and color, while honing her techniques and vision as an artist.

Eventually, Natasha returned to Mexico to raise a family. Over the ensuing years, she traveled extensively to study and exhibit her evolving work, which included creating pieces in a sub-genre of sculpture she calls "wire drawing."

In 2018 and 2019, Natasha decided to give back to the school where it all began by offering week-long workshops for students and arts faculty at Delphian, classes that spanned all grade levels. It was this work that inspired the collaboration with Heron Books to produce the *Natasha's Sketchbook* art instruction series.

The purpose is to provide simple, clear and joyful instruction in the elements of visual art. The goal is to help budding artists find the greatness of life and spirit within.

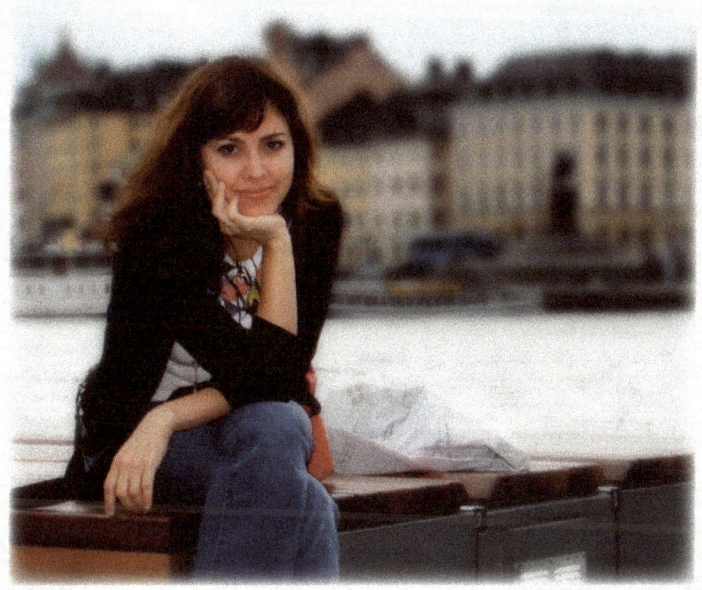

For more information visit natashagray.com.

Since 1976, Heron Books has been pioneering the development of K-12 materials that foster creative, spirited learners who can use what they have studied. Books, courses and teacher resources are developed in collaboration with its sister organization, the Delphian School®, which routinely teaches four-year-olds to read and produces high school graduates increasingly sought by top universities and corporations.

Supported by subscriber fees, charitable gifts and book sales, the mission of Heron Books is

drawing out the best in every student.

heronbooks.com

Credits:

Adobe Stock:
p. 7 abstract art #284026983
p. 13 Mayan Calendar #116944943
p. 13 Egyptian hieroglyphs #137114178
p. 19 painting "Turn at the Airport" #232077819
p. 25 Bauhaus photo #88972581
p. 28 watercolor splash #1275442471
p. 32 dip pen #266878662
p. 34 oil painting on canvas of a dancer sitting on the ground #192216786
p. 35 charcoal sticks #52266956
p. 37 Statue of Apollo Belvedere #87261697
p. 51 tea set #301799687
p. 55 drawing pencils #78792132
p. 56 drypoint #241123533
p. 60 driftwood mobile #291062125
p. 66, a. Mexican skull #287939830, b. Russian babushka dolls #39550400,
        c. Wood Elephant from India #11596140, d. Chinese jade Pixiu #273428870
p. 67 font #267255946
p. 79 The Last Supper - Leonardo da Vinci #261752112
p. 92 marble #278547098
p. 115 pigment #192901888
p. 116 pixels #221277084
p. 153 tapestry #26791918

Public domain:
p. 80 "El Rio de Luiz" by Frederic Edwin Church, Gift of the Avalon Foundation in the Public Domain
p. 83 "The Gardener's House at Antibes" by Claude Monet #930543, rawpixel.com
p. 119 "Seascape at Port-en-Bassin Normandy" by Georges Seurat ID# 2034789
p. 129 "Woman Baking Bread" by Jean-François Millet, KM 109.591

All other works are originals by Natasha Gray.

The following watercolors by Natasha Gray are interpretations of famous works:
p. 50 Girl with a Mandolin - Pablo Picasso
p. 71 Lobster Telephone - Salvador Dalí
p. 151 The Happy Donor - René Magritte
p. 152 The Holy Trinity - Andrei Rublev